MONEY-
SAVVY
KIDS

PARENTING PENNY-WISE KIDS
in a MONEY-HUNGRY WORLD

MNEY-SAVVY KIDS

J. RAYMOND ALBREKTSON

WATERBROOK
PRESS

MONEY-SAVVY KIDS
PUBLISHED BY WATERBROOK PRESS
2375 Telstar, Suite 160
Colorado Springs, Colorado 80920
A division of Random House, Inc.

Scripture taken from the *Holy Bible, New International Version*®. NIV®. Copyright ©
1973, 1978, 1984 by International Bible Society. Used by permission of Zondervan
Publishing House. All rights reserved.

Details in some anecdotes and stories have been changed to protect the identities
of the person involved.

ISBN 978-1-57856-426-2

Published in association with the literary agency of Janet Kobobel Grant,
Books & Such, 4788 Carissa Ave., Santa Rosa, CA 95405.

Library of Congress Cataloging-in-Publication Data
Albrektson, J. Raymond.
   Money-savvy kids : parenting penny-wise kids in a money-hungry world / J. Raymond Albrektson.
      p.   cm.
   ISBN 978-1-57856-426-2
      1. Wealth—Religious aspects—Christianity.   2. Money—Religious aspects—Christianity.
3. Parenting—Religious aspects—Christianity.   I. Title.

BR115.W4 A43 2001
241'.68'085—dc21

                                                                        2001045631

Printed in the United States of America
2002—First Edition

146635165

To my children, Laurie and Josh,

*from whom I never cease to learn
new and wonderful things*

CONTENTS

ACKNOWLEDGMENTS

I want to acknowledge the support and encouragement of my friends in the Plot & Blot Society: Gary Stanley, Alan Scholes, Janet Kobobel Grant, and Kirsten Wilson. Ben Franklin once wrote, "Either write something worth reading or do something worth writing." These four have encouraged me by doing both.

What We Want for Our Children

Buying eight-hundred-dollar suits and Ferragamo shoes, day-trading in his dorm room, and running up five-figure credit-card debts through betting on the outcome of NFL games—not exactly the way you expected Justin to spend the money earmarked for his college education, is it? Today's kids[1] are at greater risk than ever before of buying into the instant-wealth culture that dominates our society. The get-rich-quick mind-set and the quest for instant gratification have permeated our culture, and your family isn't immune.

Are you hoping that your kids will study hard, prepare themselves for useful careers, and then land good jobs and start families? In other words, turn into successful, financially independent adults? I thought so. But what parents hope for and what actually happens are often at odds. Check out these other, all-too-realistic scenarios.

HIGH-RISK INVESTING

Brad earned seven thousand dollars toward his college education through hard work during high school. His parents, a middle-class working couple, added considerably to that amount, but Brad ended up taking out an eight-thousand-dollar student loan to finish his senior year. That same year, Brad received a letter from a well-known brokerage firm and was invited to open an account. He parked his loan money—all eight thousand dollars—in a high-yield mutual fund growing at almost 18 percent per year.

Within two months, he decided to try for a better return from an even higher-risk investment. He had friends who helped him buy and sell a few hundred shares of stock. He made a few lucky trades and found himself suddenly two thousand dollars richer. This was too good to be true!

It wasn't long before he began making trades in companies that he knew little about. He wasn't worried though. All his friends were involved in online trading, and he was getting some great tips. Then his run of luck ended, and he lost one-third of his college loan. That's when he panicked. How could he get that money back? He heard the magic words: "Trade options! It's great. Everybody's doing it!" By Thanksgiving Brad's investment account was empty. He had no cash left to pay for winter-quarter classes.

CREDIT-CARD DEBT

Like Brad, Candace came from a middle-class background. She and her parents teamed up to pay most of her college expenses. In addition, she had received scholarships and a gift from her grandmother, so Candace had all she needed to finish her degree without taking out any student loans.

At fall registration of her freshman year, she was offered an expensive set of facial cleansers and moisturizers just for signing up for a credit card. Two years later she was maxed out on six credit cards, and her college funds were being drained just to make the minimum payments on her debt. Candace was afraid to tell her parents, and when she finally ran out of money in the spring of her junior year she owed more than twenty-eight thousand dollars in high-interest credit-card debt.

Candace had entered college debt-free and with enough money in the bank to pay for four years of college. Now she faced possibly having to quit school and move back home. She hoped she could find a job that would pay her enough so she could pay off her credit cards.

RAMPANT CONSUMERISM

Alex grew up in a family that had inherited some money. Through wise investing over twenty years, his family had actually become quite wealthy. Despite their assets, however, Alex's family lived modestly. They drove domestic cars, vacationed in Florida and Colorado rather than in Cannes and Gstaad, and tried to minimize the impact of their wealth on their children. Throughout their teenage years, Alex and his brothers worked at after-school jobs so they'd have extra spending money. None of their classmates thought of them as spoiled rich kids.

Alex had far more money than he needed to complete college because his parents had funded an investment account that enabled them (and Alex's grandparents) to make annual tax-free gifts that were designated for his education. Sadly, it was a good plan that backfired. When Alex entered college he found out how much he was worth. He soon lost interest in his studies, replacing scholarship with consumerism.

He started throwing extravagant parties for his friends, some of whom moved in with him without paying any rent. Alex didn't mind, though, since there was more money in the trust fund. He enjoyed a few more years of BMWs and Patek Philippe watches, and he traveled in style around Europe and parts of Asia. Then, completely broke, the world traveler returned home and moved back into his old room. Alex was twenty-three years old, had no financial assets, and had not a single marketable skill except his high school experience working at McDonald's.

FINANCIAL REALITIES

Do you think none of these scenarios could ever describe your children? After all, you're teaching them not just positive values but biblical values. You're doing your best to raise them to be godly adults who will live wisely and well when they finally leave the nest.

It's good to do all those things, but unfortunately it's not enough. The biggest, most powerful marketing machine in history has targeted your children in an attempt to turn them into "model consumers"—the kind who are easy prey to slick advertising campaigns. The persuasive power of marketing and the appeal of ever-changing fashion work together to dwarf your influence as a parent. The goal of this faceless consortium of advertisers, retailers, and trendsetters is to train your offspring to spend everything they have, everything you have, and everything you both might earn in the future on *their* products, preferably on credit.

How can you even begin to compete with the thousands of ads on television and billboards and in magazines that your children see every day of their lives? Even if your kids are still toddlers, you already know the potential for manipulating their little minds. Every time a preschooler pleads, "Mommy! Buy me one of these," a group of marketing moguls exchanges high-fives. They're celebrating because they're one step closer to separating your children from their (that is, your) money.

That's the bad news. But there is still plenty of good news to be had. In spite of our consumer culture that has targeted your innocent children, you are still in a position to raise your kids to be godly and wise adults. It won't be easy, and to succeed you'll need a clear plan. But with persistence and the right approach, you can train your kids to become adults who are independent, debt-free, and capable of wisely managing their finances. If you do nothing, however, your children can look forward to a lifetime of financial manipulation—much of it with your money—with little likelihood of achieving happy and successful lives.

A WORKABLE PLAN

When it comes to developing the best plan for training our children, the place to begin is the Bible. The Bible is loaded with practical advice for parents who hope to raise money-smart yet unspoiled children. We want to use the most effective methods available to pound wisdom into the little skulls of our beloved offspring. Wisdom that is grounded in the Bible leads to the development of character. And character, as expressed in the parry and thrust of everyday life, is exactly what our kids will need in order to navigate a safe course through the financial reefs of adulthood.

In this book you'll learn a simple five-step program to give your children the best possible chance to become the kind of money-savvy adults you want them to be. The task, in a nutshell, is to teach them five essential values about money and its proper uses. These core values are hard work, generous giving, wise saving, careful spending, and limited borrowing—and then only with great fear and trembling. These values, if laced together with a strong biblical emphasis on building character, are the tools every child needs in order to arrive at adulthood equipped to deal with the realities of the modern world.

When my children were preschoolers, I often told them, "Remember, your parents are your *most important* teachers!" I hoped that during the years our kids were in school, Kathy and I would retain some credibility with them when they were exposed to ideas and values that conflicted with biblical values. As parents responsible to train our children, we need to teach them attitudes (about God's purposes for work, money, and leisure) as well as skills (simple math, balancing accounts, evaluating a variety of loans and investments). But—a crucial condition—our children's financial education must occur within a framework of character development, especially self-control. If a child can decide to defer a short-term pleasure in favor of a more significant yet distant desire, or save for a specific purchase despite the temptations to buy it on credit, we can be sure that child is on the way to a successful adult life.

If you follow the guidelines in this book, can you really be sure that your children will be able to resist the lures of easy credit, materialism, debt, and other financial enticements of our go-for-the-gusto society? What if your children are already teenagers? Is it too late for these principles to work for them? Some children will make bad choices no matter how they've been trained. They have a free will—definitely a mixed blessing. With that in mind, I'll explain how to structure your finances to minimize the damage of your kids' unwise decisions and to preserve second chances.

Don't let the possibility of future mistakes—yours or your kids'—keep you from taking positive action. By far the most dangerous course of all is to do nothing. Don't assume your children will just naturally learn how to wisely manage their money. They won't move into adulthood surrounded by encouraging voices emphasizing the wisdom of saving, the peril of indebtedness, the earthly pleasures of meaningful work. A far more sinister chorus is already chanting much more dangerous messages into their ears:

"Work is what you do when you can't afford to do anything else."

"You deserve a new car—and we can fit payments to any income!"

"Somebody's got to win the big jackpot...and you sure can't win unless you play!"

"Buy-and-hold investing is for saps. The real money is in options!"

"You're still using that old computer? Get a new one and donate that antique to the Smithsonian."

Have you bought into any of these messages? You know you have, and you're a mature adult! If you find yourself constantly being manipulated to abandon biblical values in favor of instant gratification, imagine how vulnerable your children are. They need your guidance, and that's why aggressive action is called for. You really can help your children learn biblical values. True, you may need to take a refresher course, but education becomes all the more vivid when you're learning the same lessons you're teaching your children. The really important thing is to roll up your sleeves and get started.

When I was only six, I managed to climb almost twelve feet into a large willow tree bordering my grandmother's property. Once up there, I lost my confidence and decided I wouldn't even try to climb down. When dinnertime came and went, my father finally discovered my predicament. He offered a simple solution: Hang from the branch and drop, and he would catch me. I cried with fear, unwilling to take the plunge. But as the night grew dusky and the crickets began to chirp, the disadvantage of doing nothing dawned on me. I eventually jumped, and when safely in my father's arms, I wondered why I had been so fearful.

So gather your courage and leap with me into the exciting challenge of raising our children into godly, money-savvy, debt-phobic, unspoiled adults. We'll begin by looking at what it takes for parents to model wise financial practices in front of their children.

PART I

PREPARING TO
MENTOR YOUR KIDS

Chapter 1

Hope for the Financially Flawed

Your Kids Can Learn from Your Mistakes

One of the most colorful characters of the Roaring Twenties was Wrong-Way Corrigan, a maverick pilot in the age of aerial daredevils and barnstormers. Corrigan made his reputation by flying solo from New York to Ireland. The only catch was that the U.S. government had banned all solo transatlantic flights after a rash of fatalities following Charles Lindbergh's successful New York–Paris flight.

Wrong-Way made the New York–Ireland flight anyway. When challenged, he simply pointed out that it was all a mistake. He had intended to fly from New York to Los Angeles and had simply read his compass backward.

As parents, sometimes we feel a lot like Wrong-Way Corrigan. We have a clear goal in mind, a daring goal, actually. We want to raise our children in such a way that they will grow into godly adults. But too often we don't have a clue how to get from here to there. We sometimes wonder who *we* are to be building character into our children when we've cut so many corners ourselves. And when it comes to finances, how can we raise our children to be wise and capable money managers when we feel so inadequate in those areas ourselves?

GOD PROVIDES THE TOOLS

Just over three thousand years ago an angel paid a surprise visit to a young Israelite named Gideon. He was so terrified of the Midianite raiders who plagued Israel that he was reduced to winnowing his grain inside the shelter of a winepress. That's like trying to fly a kite in a barrel, and not a particularly efficient method of separating grain from chaff. The angel knew of Gideon's misgivings and greeted him with these words: "The LORD is with you, mighty warrior" (Judges 6:12).

Gideon was a guy who had flaws and insecurities like the rest of us. In fact, he was probably all too well acquainted with his own inadequacies. Gideon had focused on his weaknesses while God saw his potential. If we read further in Judges, we'll see that this self-conscious young man who took to a winepress in fear later became a military leader of Israel. The personal transformation evident in Gideon's life proves God's unique capability to take our human weaknesses and give us what we need to prosper.

One story in particular highlights God's talent in this area. In Judges 7:1-7, the army of Israel was anticipating a battle against the superior forces of the Midianites. In opposition to all known logic, God instructed Gideon to *send home* the bulk of his army so that only a few hundred warriors were left. But that's not all. Instead of arming themselves with spears, shields, swords, and bows, God directed the Israelites to go to war against the fierce Midianites carrying lamps, clay pots, and trumpets!

Everything that Gideon could have used to fight the Midianites—namely a large, well-equipped army—was taken away. Put yourself in Gideon's place. Even with shrewd military tactics, how could you be expected to defeat a well-trained enemy when your forces were armed with nothing more threatening than clay pots and rams' horns? But if you read the account of this battle in Judges 7, you'll see that a small Israelite force bearing no traditional weapons routed the forces of Midian.

Why am I telling you a story about Old Testament warfare? It's to give you courage as you try to raise financially smart children, especially if you're doubting that you have a single financially savvy bone in your body. Like Gideon's getting the job done with too few soldiers and no conventional weapons, God wouldn't call you to do something without fully equipping you for the job.

When we send Justin outdoors to pull weeds, we know he has everything he needs to do the job—two strong arms and a free summer afternoon. But *he* may not think so. He might walk out into that vast expanse of grass, flower beds, and shrubbery and feel completely overwhelmed. In the same way, we need to reflect on the truth that God has indeed given us what we need to raise children of character who will become financially wise and responsible adults. He has given us the tools; it's up to us to identify and use them.

YOUR NUMBER-ONE ASSET

If God provides the tools you'll need, what are they? There are several, including an honest self-appraisal, commitment to the task, and the faith to trust God with the results. But God also provides another crucial asset: motivation. You wouldn't be reading this book unless God's Spirit was creating within you a desire to raise godly children. And if you hope to succeed in this venture, you have to keep that motivation alive for the long haul.

You can't do without it—it's like the flour in a cake, the rubber in tires, or the spark in your car's ignition system. You'll need other assets, but the rest are minor compared with this one. If you feel your motivation flagging, consider the consequences of *not* training your children to be financially savvy. I have two words for you: "boomerang kids." When your children are grown, you really do want them to leave the nest and build nests of their own. You want them to possess the godly character that produces mature, balanced, self-supporting adults.

Not long ago my daughter married a fine young man. Preparing to help my only daughter pledge herself to another man was a bittersweet period. But every time my wife, Kathy, mentioned how empty our nest had become, I couldn't help reflecting that it was far superior to the alternative. Of course we hope to remain close to our adult children, but we don't want to be summoned to rescue them from a financial tarpit. We welcome them to visit us, but not because they're looking for free groceries and a cheap place to sleep.

No parent wants boomerang kids. Our goal is to build character and financial skills into our children's lives so they can succeed both as people and as wise stewards of their finances. As our kids grow, teaching them the skills and values of wise financial management will help ground them in godly character. As I'll show in later chapters, character development and training in good money habits go hand in hand. By giving our children a character-based financial education we will furnish them with the tools they'll need to live successfully as adults.

DON'T SWEAT PAST MISTAKES

Perhaps you hear a nagging voice inside your head telling you that you just don't have what it takes. "You're a financial loser!" whines your inner wimp. Other voices join the chorus: "Remember all that credit-card debt? Did you forget those moronic 'investments' you made? And your checkbook is a disgrace!"

Three words of advice: Ignore those voices. You're an adult, you're motivated, and you're reading this book. Together we'll discover everything you need to train your children in the skills of wise money management. If you feel like you're being thrown into the deep end of the pool without water wings, you're in good company. Even physicians are trained in a similar process. A doctor once told me that when it came to learning how to perform an appendectomy, for example, the rule was "watch one, do one, teach one."

We've all made financial decisions that we wish we could take back. We can look at our past mistakes as great opportunities for wisdom development for ourselves *and* for our kids. With age comes experience, both good and bad. So we should convert our firsthand knowledge into wisdom by reflecting on the biblical principles we violated and making the right midcourse correction. I'd guess that every surgeon who has sweated bullets through a touch-

PREPARING TO MENTOR YOUR KIDS

and-go operation learned far more from that experience than from performing a textbook example of surgery.

A QUICK SELF-APPRAISAL

You're motivated, and you're not going to let previous financial failures keep you from teaching your kids to succeed. But before moving on, you might want to consider a little housecleaning. What are the financial habits that you want to teach your children that you might not be modeling yourself?

You'll want to teach your kids to fear indebtedness the way a burned child fears a hot stove, right? Take a hard look at your own debt situation. If you're regularly paying finance charges on credit-card debt, take a swig of your own medicine before you try to dose your kids with it. Even if you only have one credit card with ongoing finance charges, try this simple strategy for debt reduction.

Find an ugly, scratchy, moldy piece of old rope, the funkier the better. A length of rusty iron chain is actually superior, because it more vividly symbolizes the slavery of indebtedness. (The drawback is that it sets off metal detectors.) Now tie a hunk of that nasty rope around your ankle. Tie additional lengths of rope until you have as many revolting ankle bracelets as you have overdue credit-card balances. Finally, cut each rope off your ankle *only* when you've paid off a credit card.

Sound extreme? If you had to wear ropes around your ankle—in the shower, at work, at the gym, and even in bed—you'd quickly learn to hate debt just as you want your kids to hate it. When little Justin asks, "Mom and Dad, why are you wearing a smelly rope around your ankles?" you can explain that you have become enslaved to debt because it exerts a power over you that you can't control without eliminating it altogether.

The point is this: If you have consumer debt, now's the time to get on top of it. But that's not the entire answer. You also need to model generosity, disciplined savings, and wise spending habits. You want your children to become adults who give generously, save wisely, and spend carefully. The key to success is to raise them in a home where you model these same values. If this doesn't yet characterize your own money habits, there's no time like now to start making changes. The goal is to live on less than you earn, so that the difference between income and expenses can flow into giving and savings. As I explained in a previous book, *Living Large: How to Live Well—Even on a Little,*[1] your target is to structure your finances so that you give some, save some, and live joyfully on the rest. This can become your own financial guiding light as well as the principle that directs your children.

If you're climbing out from under years of poor financial habits, you have the raw material to help provide your kids with a dose of reality they would never experience in an "ideal" family situation. Your checkbook might be the financial version of Wrong-Way Corrigan, but there's nothing like raising children to motivate us adults to get our act together.

After all, Wrong-Way became famous for a single spectacular example of poor navigation. He didn't make it a practice to fly from San Francisco to Los Angeles by way of Seattle. If we want to build character in our children, we need to develop our own financial navigational skills. At least we know the ultimate goal—

building godly character that will enable our kids to succeed as adults. The challenge now is how to get from here to there.

In the next chapter we'll see that God has already given us the means. For starters, think of raising money-savvy kids as the world's biggest game of Monopoly. Let's get out the game board, pick our tokens (I like the racecar best), and get ready to play.

Money Management and Godly Character

Winning at the Game of Life

Not long ago a friend of mine returned from a scuba-diving trip to the Micronesian island of Yap. After getting a full report on the fabulous diving he'd done there, I joked, "And did you bring me anything for my coin collection?" He laughed, recognizing that the traditional currency of the Yapese islanders consists of huge, mostly immobile stones—some as large as truck tires. On the island of Yap, when they say "you can't take it with you," it's true of this life as well as the next.

Wealth—even the kind that fits into a wallet—is like that. We didn't bring it into the world, even if we were born into a wealthy family. We certainly can't take it out of this world. So the question is this: While we're here, what do we do with our money? And how can we teach our children to use it wisely?

If you've been financially blessed, you face the challenge of raising unspoiled children who won't take their unearned wealth for granted. If you're struggling financially or coping with the consequences of past financial mistakes, you want to help your children make better decisions than you did. In either case, how can you begin to lay a foundation that will carry your children confidently into an uncertain future?

In one of Jesus' most misunderstood parables, a rascally manager embezzled from his master's wealth in order to gain the friendship of his master's debtors (Luke 16:1-13). The manager gave away what he couldn't possibly keep (and, in fact, didn't even own) in order to gain something he could not lose—the gratitude and friendship of those whose debts he reduced. In telling that story Jesus emphasized that wealth is temporary, something very much like the play money in the game of Monopoly. The steward knew he was playing with someone else's cash, so he used it shrewdly while he still had access to it.

The financial assets you "own" are just like Monopoly money. Those bits of pink and yellow paper only have value while you're playing the game. You can buy railroads and real estate, pay your taxes and rent, and even bail yourself out of jail. But as soon as the game is over, the Monopoly money is nothing more than colorful pieces of paper.

Wouldn't it be great if we could somehow transform that great pile of Monopoly money into wealth that lasts beyond the game? That's exactly the opportunity that stands before us. By teaching our kids to appropriately value and manage the money that comes their way, we can build something of lasting value—our children's character. In that respect they'll be way ahead of the scoundrel in

Jesus' parable, but they'll also acquire his wisdom in spending money that is temporarily available to them in order to achieve permanent results.

TRAINING IN GODLY CHARACTER

Character is a concept that has fallen out of fashion in our culture. Celebrities are described as great actors, superb athletes, winsome politicians, or shrewd investors. When was the last time you read about a movie star's sterling character? Yet character represents the inward superstructure on which the outer person is constructed. Without it one is spiritually empty, a hollow shell of a person, one who lives without authenticity or true purpose.

The concept of character for the Christian should be even more clearly understood. For believers, character is based on the reality of God's rule in our lives. We have personal value because God chose to ransom us by paying an inconceivable price, the life of his Son. Our lives have meaning because we were created to live in eternal fellowship with God. Developing a Christian character means growing spiritually so that God's values become our values. Since our outward choices reflect our inner values, as we grow in character we reach a point where the choices we make are consistent with God's values.

Developing Christian character is no small thing, and apart from God's work through the Holy Spirit, we'll never be able to create it in our children. It's a lifelong process of learning and being transformed by the work of God. But parents play a crucial role in setting our children on a course of life transformation, starting in their formative years. Then we help them move forward in the development of Christian character. As they advance into adolescence, more and more of the responsibility for character formation shifts onto their shoulders. But even then we can help them build a godly character—if we know how.

THE TRUE VALUE OF MONEY

When children play Monopoly, they learn how play money mimics the use of real money. Likewise, when children play with real money, they learn how earthly wealth imitates the use of spiritual wealth. If we allow our kids to grow up believing that everyday wealth (property, assets, material possessions) is of ultimate value, we've kept them from understanding the real significance of wealth. Our children need to understand that money is important because it can be used to achieve great good, especially in God's kingdom.

As we teach our kids that money is not the ultimate goal, we can use money as a tool in chiseling a lasting outline onto the somewhat blank slates that younger children represent. If we are successful, they will view money with more of an eternal perspective, putting long-range needs ahead of short-term gratification.

Remember when you were a teenager? Fashion defined certain groups and often determined who was "in" and who was "out." It's no less true today. Every teenager wants to belong, so it's no surprise that teens are susceptible to peer pressure. When everybody is wearing a particular brand of (horrendously expensive) clothing, it takes character to refuse to buy into that fad. Perfectly good clothing can be bought for much less money, and the cash that is saved can be put to better use in a college savings fund.

But designer clothing is just the tip of the iceberg. Most teenagers crave their own cars and will make almost any sacrifice to get one. More kids take part-time jobs to cover auto expenses than for any other reason. It takes character for an adolescent to drive mom's car—and to save hard-earned wages for a short-term mission trip instead.

Character is what it takes to do the right thing even when there are powerful temptations to do something else. This is true with money management and with all of life. The same kids who are making decisions on expensive designer clothing and flashy cars may also be experiencing strong urges to experiment with sex. Character is what helps a teenager draw appropriate boundaries.

Of course, opportunities to take the wrong road don't end with the teenage years. Later in life every young man and woman will be pressured to take a short cut to "the good life" through unwise borrowing or unethical means such as cheating on taxes. Again, character helps a person make the right choices.

TAKING THE LONG VIEW

When it comes to money management, character means putting off short-term pleasure in favor of achieving a far more important long-term goal. In other words, financial character is grounded in the concept of deferred gratification. The choices we make today either help us reach our long-term goals or make it next to impossible. And those outward choices are indicators of inner character. (We'll discuss the principle of deferred gratification in greater depth in later chapters.)

How do we use wise money management to teach godly

character? A good starting point is to help our children see that money has value only in this life. In the game of Monopoly, the bank gives every player a financial stake. We need to help our children understand that our wealth, whether inherited or earned, was given to us by our heavenly Father. And just as the Monopoly money goes back in the box at the end of the game, the money we possess is merely in our temporary care.

Our children need to understand that money is ours to use, not to own. In Monopoly, the players don't literally "own" the houses, hotels, and railroads. Those objects are merely part of playing the game. Likewise in life, God owns everything, and he lends his riches to us for our temporary use. The apostle Paul emphasized this when writing his young disciple, Timothy, urging him to "command those who are rich in this present world not to…put their hope in wealth…but to put their hope in God, who richly provides us with everything for our enjoyment" (1 Timothy 6:17).

That's a good thing, because we can trust our loving Father to use his wealth to care for us. And since it's God's money and not ours, we can rest in the knowledge that financial failure is not the ultimate catastrophe.

As we help our children learn to use money wisely, they'll make mistakes. (Haven't we all?) But to teach wise financial management, we have to allow our kids to truly handle the money. You don't go very far in a game of Monopoly without actually handling the deeds, the little houses and hotels, and the rental fees. Children should be introduced to money appropriately at every stage in their lives. They need to grow accustomed to making their own financial decisions. Not all of those choices will prove to be wise ones, of course. And while it hurts us to see our children make blunders, it's an essential part of the learning process. If we do our jobs carefully, we can limit the damage and scope of some of those goofs, or at least make the learning experience worth the price of the lesson.

EVERYONE SUCCEEDS

The goal in the game of Monopoly is simple—to bankrupt the other players. This is where real-life financial training varies from the game. In life, our own success contributes to the success of those around us. A young child with a few dollars has three options. He can spend it (candy, toys, books), save it (piggy bank, savings account), or give it away (missions, humanitarian needs). Even young children need to realize that their choices are significant and can make a real difference in their future (through wise saving and careful spending) and in the lives of others (through giving).

Most children strongly identify with the story of the loaves and the fishes as told in John's gospel (6:5-13). The disciples were utterly at a loss when Jesus proposed that they somehow feed the hungry multitude. The only bright spot just then was a small boy whose five barley loaves and two small fish were used by Jesus to meet the need of the great crowd. That small gift not only fed the multitude, but also illustrated the enormous impact that a single child can have when his or her meager assets are put into the Lord's hands.

Although we can't know for sure, I like to imagine what the parents of that little boy were like. By any standard, the family was probably poor. The child's lunch was that of a peasant, and not a well-off peasant at that. Yet it appears that his parents had enriched him more than they realized. As far as we know, he gave up his lunch when there were plenty of other options. Perhaps he struggled over his own hunger and considered keeping his lunch for himself. Or he could have saved his food and shared it with just a few friends. But he gave away his entire lunch, holding nothing back. His act of generosity still inspires us two thousand years later.

Like the parents of the boy in the New Testament story, we want our own kids to practice generosity. When we're instilling Christian character, though, we need to recognize that no two kids are alike. So how can we customize our training to take advantage of each child's particular strengths? While the goal is constant—to build character while teaching money-management skills—there are several different routes that will take us there. In the next chapter we'll take out our yardsticks and calipers and see which route works best for each unique child.

Chapter 3

Each Kid Is Different

Take Advantage of Your Child's Unique Bent

I don't know many people who have felt drawn to insects as household pets, but when I was ten I couldn't help it. A praying mantis had taken up residence near our patio, and I spent much of that summer observing it. I discovered, for instance, that this particular praying mantis was a picky eater. I would catch various "prey" and dangle them in front of the treasured insect—never once getting it to take a bite out of my proffered meals.

But even a mantis has to eat. Every once in a while a honeybee would buzz nearby, and the praying mantis would become even more motionless than usual. If the honeybee flew within range, the mantis would whip its arms around the bee's body. Buzzing frantically, the doomed bee would be manipulated until the mantis had one arm around the bee's head, which the mantis would unscrew like the lid on a pickle jar and discard.

The mantis would then reach inside the bee and scoop out its innards, munching away until nothing remained but an empty yellowish skin. Apart from my delight at watching such a spectacle, I couldn't help but notice that the mantis would disregard many other available meals in order to capture the one it really wanted. It would completely ignore flies, wasps, and ladybugs. But let a tasty bee buzz nearby, and the praying mantis would soon be enjoying its chosen delicacy. In other words, even a dumb insect had mastered the concept of deferred gratification.

BUILDING ON NATURAL ABILITIES

All children have the potential to resist an immediate pleasure for the sake of a later, far superior benefit. Some, however, find it extremely difficult to resist something they really want—right now! We don't get to custom-order our children, so we have to recognize which aspects of financial training are most likely to have the biggest impact on each child. Some children are naturally gifted to save for future needs or desires. But for most, deferred gratification is something that needs to be carefully nurtured. Consider the cases of Zachary and Alyssa, who come close to defining the spectrum of how children approach the future.

Zachary's teachers agree that he's a great kid but not the most organized kid in the world. If he's given an allowance, he's likely to lose it before he gets a chance to spend it. If by some miracle his money doesn't get run through the washing machine in his jeans pocket, it's almost certain to wind up in the first coin slot that catches his eye. It could be a video game or a machine dispensing overpriced gumballs or disgusting rubber reptiles.

Not only does Zachary have trouble keeping track of his money, he's also prone to give it away. Whether he loses his money, spends it, or shares it with a friend, he's happy and doesn't seem to mind that others take advantage of his generosity. Zachary often finds toys that he'd like to buy, but he seldom purchases any item that costs more than whatever random change happens to be in his pocket.

Alyssa, on the other hand, is a natural-born saver. She holds on to practically every birthday check she receives. When she gets an allowance, she saves most of it and often coaxes others into providing what she has the means to buy for herself. Sometimes Alyssa considers using some of her money to purchase a toy, but on reflection she decides to just hang on to the cash. Her siblings know she has money, but they also know she's seldom willing to lend it. And when she does make a loan, she keeps track of every penny that is owed her.

We've all probably encountered children like Zachary or Alyssa. They illustrate the innate variability in children's attitudes toward money. Zachary takes no thought for the future. He exists in an eternal present in which future needs are unreal or irrelevant. Alyssa takes no thought for the present. She holds on to as much of her money as possible so she can preserve every possible future option.

THE SHAPE OF SUCCESS

According to the Bible, parents have the privilege of training their children for success in the future (Proverbs 22:6). Just as young shrubs can be shaped into spheres, cones, and sometimes even the forms of animals, so children can also be shaped—within certain limits. The catch is to find the natural direction of the child and encourage him to develop a shape appropriate to his nature.

It's tempting to look at Zachary's disregard for hoarding his pennies and try to inculcate a "save for a rainy day" philosophy. While it's true that Zachary probably needs to grow in that regard, a wise parent will recognize that he will always be generous with his money and oriented more to the present than the future. He can be taught much that will help him value the future uses of money, but no amount of training is going to turn him into a clone of Alyssa.

And it would be a shame to do so, as he has such obvious strengths. It was probably a boy like Zachary who provided the loaves and fishes that were multiplied to feed the crowds that gathered to hear Jesus preach. Zachary's great strength is his openhandedness and his general lack of selfishness. This natural inclination can be put to great use if he is taught how to marshal his resources for philanthropy. Just as he spends freely and gives freely as a child, Zachary could grow into one whose openhandedness could be used to benefit multitudes of people who need help.

Alyssa, on the other hand, has little need for instruction in preparing for her future financial needs. Her challenge is to recognize a worthy goal toward which her natural tendencies can be directed. She has the potential for amassing wealth, but she needs direction in the real purpose of possessions and how to eventually put them to their best uses.

As parents we seem to have built-in microscopes that enlarge our children's faults and weaknesses. But we often have blind spots when we gaze upon their greatest strengths. We need to ask ourselves how our children's basic natures can best be molded into wise, capable, financially competent adults. We're never going to turn our child's greatest fault into his or her strongest feature. So rather than focusing on the negatives, we should strive to identify and build upon the positives. If we do our best to ensure that we've laid a solid foundation in the bricks and mortar of a godly character, we're halfway there. If we can at the same time nurture a mind-set that bypasses short-term amusements for real long-term satisfaction, we can give ourselves a hearty pat on the back.

Before we get too self-congratulatory, though, we need to remember that, as parents, we're always in the mode of training children by modeling good habits. Our own attitudes and practices will have a much bigger impact on our children than any lessons we try to teach them. Are we modeling daily disciplines that make it possible to set aside assets now that will be available to cover future financial needs? That's deferred gratification in action.

A top priority for today's savings and investments is a college fund for our children. In the next chapter we'll find out what it's going to take to put the kids through State U.

Chapter 4

I Am Justin's College Fund

The Sooner You Start, the Less Scary It Will Be

When I travel outside the United States, I miss the easy availability
of strong coffee in large containers more than any other convenience of my native land. At home in California I can go to my
favorite coffee shop and soon be sipping a sixteen-ounce mug of
Redlands blend or organic Chiapas or any number of other delicious coffees. (I'm writing these words from the middle of nowhere
in the central mountains of southern Bulgaria and would pay
almost any price for a big thermal mug of delicious coffee.)

Recently I was chatting with a friend at my favorite coffee shop
about two of my favorite subjects—coffee and financial wisdom.
Mike is a young married guy with a pregnant wife. He has two
more years of study at a nearby medical school before beginning
several more years of internship and residency. We began to talk
about the future, and Mike expressed considerable anxiety about

paying off his student loans while simultaneously saving up to cover the future college expenses of his kids.

I asked Mike what he was drinking, and it turned out that he tended to begin his afternoon studies with a mocha latte followed up by a booster cup of house blend a few hours later. The total cost of these afternoon beverages ran about four and a half bucks a day. I pointed out that if Mike could afford that kind of coffee habit, he could certainly afford to save for at least one child's college education.

Mike's daily expenditure of $4.50 could easily be set aside in a college savings fund for his soon-to-be-born baby. That small amount, added every day to an interest-bearing account, will cover most or even all of the college expenses for a student eighteen years from now. I won't ask you to do the math, since I have financial calculators built into the computer program I use to manage my personal finances. Allow me to plug in a few figures and see if my college-fund assertion really stands up.

COLLEGE ON TWO CUPS A DAY

Mike was spending close to $5.00 a day on his caffeine habit. Medical students tell me this isn't a luxury but a nonnegotiable aspect of completing their grueling program. But let's say that Mike took a similar amount ($4.50) and put it in a shoebox every day. At the end of each week he'd have $31.50. We'll make that Mike's weekly contribution to his child's college fund. It doesn't sound like much, I know, but bear with me. Let's say Mike's son is born on schedule and eighteen years later little Mike Jr. will be headed off to college.

If Mike invests $31.50 each week in a mutual fund that averages the annual rate of return of the U.S. stock market for the last thirty years (about 12 percent), he would be looking at a college fund of about $1,738 at the end of his first year. That's not bad, considering it's the result of socking away just a few bucks a day. On the other hand, Mike could grow discouraged, thinking that this amount wouldn't even pay the book bill for Mike Jr.'s first year at Harvard. But hang on. Things get interesting really fast. After a couple of years of systematic investing, the numbers begin to add up dramatically.

By the time Mike Jr. enters kindergarten at age five, his college fund has already surpassed $11,200. By the time little Mikey's a bona fide teenager (at thirteen), it has surged to more than $51,000. By the time he's eighteen and ready to head off to Harvard, his dad's mocha latte fund has grown to an astounding $104,416. Most of us would say that at the modest cost of just $31.50 per week, Mike Jr.'s college situation is well in hand.

THE EFFECTS OF INFLATION

"But wait just a minute, Mr. Know-It-All!" cries out the observant reader. "What about inflation?"

Excellent question. The cost of higher education is sure to increase before Mike Jr. leaves for college, and the value of the dollar—if history is any guide—will continue to decline. So let me, in the spirit of integrity, factor in the effects of inflation. I'll assume a 4 percent annual rate of inflation. To be fair, though, the cost of a mocha latte will also increase. So to keep things stable, let's say

Mike increases the weekly contribution to his mutual fund at a percentage rate equal to the rise in inflation.

The math is a bit more difficult, but my computer's financial calculator can handle it. Because of inflation, Mike Jr. will have fewer inflation-adjusted dollars available for his education. But how much will that be? Pause for drum roll... His education funds adjusted for inflation will be $135,047. But in terms of current dollars that amounts to only about half as much, or $65,753. Assuming the money is doled out over a four-year period, and that the amount that isn't spent each year continues to grow at our assumed interest rate of 12 percent, that works out to about $18,300 per year.

It looks like Mike Jr. will still be in pretty good shape when he reaches college age. And maybe my assumptions are too conservative. Nobody knows if a new investment boom will result in more rapid growth of these college assets. The opposite could also happen, of course, but here's my point: Money grows over time, and the sooner you start and the more frequently you add to it, the larger the amount at the end.

Some of you already have the finances you'll need to accomplish major goals such as educating your children or providing for your own retirement needs. Even if you don't need to start investing now for little Justin's education, he needs to see you start doing it. A parent who models disciplined saving and wise investing is teaching his or her children a priceless lesson. And who knows what you'll need the money for in the future?

Children need to know that financial success in the future—whether it's having the money to replace a decrepit automobile, taking the family to Disney World, or financing a college education for three kids—takes planning, foresight, and weekly discipline starting today. We aren't doing our children any favors when we shield them completely from the financial realities of life. Sure, they need to know that their home and their parents' love and care are dead-bang certainties. And they really don't need to have dad come home and announce, "Well, they fired me! Don't have a clue where the next paycheck's coming from." That kind of adult grief shouldn't be inflicted on younger children.

On the other hand, children need to observe realistic models, including financial models, of responsible adulthood. Seeing parents systematically (and successfully) saving and investing for long-term goals is an important way to develop in your children that Holy Grail of financial responsibility, the ability to defer gratification.

All children have the potential to resist an immediate pleasure in order to enjoy a delayed superior benefit. Some, however, find it extremely difficult. This urge to immediately obtain the object of our desire can single-handedly doom any person to a life of financial failure—whether it's not having the money to educate your children or being short on funds to replace your house's leaky roof.

Adults struggle with deferring gratification just as children do. Instead of a video game that has us reaching for our wallet it's a new computer or an SUV or a Caribbean cruise. If we're going to succeed at preparing our children to resist lures like these, we've got to start resisting them ourselves. The basis of a solid financial future can't be left to chance. It has to be built on the ability to defer gratification. And a great way to practice this discipline is to set up an investment fund that we contribute to on a regular basis—weekly or monthly is best. Planning for our kids' education can help us practice the self-control we need in other areas of financial management, including spending, saving, and giving. The added benefit is that our consistent example is a convincing model for our kids as we train them to do the same as they grow to maturity.

Maybe you have accumulated significant consumer debt, and you really haven't given much thought to how your children will finish their education. Surely you can afford the cash equivalent of a mocha latte a day! And when times are tough, the discipline of saving for an important long-term goal makes an even deeper impression on your impressionable child. "Wow," he thinks, "I must be important, and my education also."

Even if you're financially able to fund your children's college education out of existing assets, why should you pass up such a great opportunity to teach them about the value of money invested over time? Why neglect teaching them about consistency, discipline, and purposeful saving toward important goals? As a wise man once said in Proverbs 30:25, "Ants are creatures of little strength, yet they store up their food in the summer." Make it a goal that your kids will be at least as wise about saving as ants appear to be.

Of course, you wouldn't have money to invest if you didn't head off to work every day. And that holds true for kids as they enter adolescence. In fact, it starts at a much younger age with helping out around the house. In the next chapter we'll talk about helping kids learn to value the "W" word and to see it as an essential part of life. And as usual, you'll have your own opportunity to do a little attitude adjustment in the process.

PART II

PRINCIPLE 1: WORK HARD

Chapter 5

"Work" Isn't a Dirty Word

Finding Its Meaning and Value

What's the greatest job in the world? Here are my top three: ice-cream flavor designer for Ben & Jerry's, underwater photographer for *Skin Diving* magazine, and international speaker/teacher. But what if you're allergic to milk products, the thought of swimming with sharks brings on a sudden attack of hydrophobia, and the only thing that terrifies you more than sharks is having to speak in public?

My idea of ideal jobs might not be yours. So what defines the perfect job? According to a former student, "The coolest job in the world is doing exactly what you love." He came very close to the mark. The perfect job for any of us is one that doesn't feel like work.

Ah, work! It's easily one of the most abused four-letter words in the English language. How can we keep our kids from seeing this honorable investment of skills and energy as something other than a necessary evil? Let me take that a step further: How can we teach our children that work is one of God's blessings and not the daily curse that our culture says it is?

Even Christians often need a realignment of their thinking when it comes to the topic of work. I've actually seen jaws drop when I point out to students that God invented work before sin corrupted our environment, and that it was evidently meant to be a *highly pleasurable* activity.

Consider Genesis 2:15: "The LORD God took the man and put him in the Garden of Eden to work it and take care of it." Adam had a job before he had a wife, and he was working long before sin contaminated all the good things God had made. Sadly, the fall of Adam and Eve led to a drastic change in working conditions. "Cursed is the ground because of you; through painful toil you will eat of it all the days of your life" (Genesis 3:17). While this passage makes the point that work devolved into a painful necessity, it also indicates that God's plan for humankind still included work.

A CONTAGIOUS ATTITUDE

One practical aspect of the Christian message is that when a person is in Christ, "he is a new creation; the old has gone, the new has come!" (2 Corinthians 5:17). And one of the blessings of being a new creation is the possibility of developing new attitudes toward work. While we can't perfectly re-create the pristine joy that Adam found working in God's garden, we can still bring new attitudes to our daily tasks. Do we want our children to work with eagerness and delight? We can help build that approach into their lives.

As you think about this process, remember that your own attitudes toward work rub off on your kids. You might think your job is simply to train your kids how to work. The catch is that the most effective training mode for children is modeling. That which you model consistently in your own life—whether for good or bad—is very likely to be imitated by your children.

Do you remember your parents trying to convince you that some despised vegetable was really yummy? They'd put the detestable squash, spinach, or lima beans in their own mouths, roll their eyes in feigned enchantment, and swallow delightedly in hopes that you'd do the same. Fat chance! Kids aren't deceived by the occasional parental performance, but they are impressed by long-term attitudes that are evidenced naturally in their parents' lifestyles. So if you want to teach your kids to like work, start by evaluating your own attitudes. Do you regard work as one of God's blessings, embraced joyfully and thankfully? And if so, does it show? If your car wears a bumper sticker reading, "The worst day fishing beats the best day working," you're sending your kids a message you will probably regret.

Some of the saddest images of the twentieth century are those scratchy newsreels from the Great Depression showing long lines of workmen with no jobs. Those men wore their despair on their faces. Their hope had evaporated along with their employment. Work had meaning for the Depression-era generation that surpassed a paycheck that put food on the table. They found dignity and meaning in the practice of their skills.

It's no surprise to anyone that things are far different today. A strong back and a willing heart are no longer adequate qualifications for a person to find meaningful work in our high-tech society.

And believe me, no amount of government support or social services can make a person feel complete when his labor isn't valued. When our culture doesn't support a biblical value, such as the dignity of work, it's doubly important for parents to model that value at home.

WHY WORK MATTERS

The starting point in teaching your kids to value work is to value it yourself. Sure, it puts food on the table, but it's more than that—it's an integral part of God's plan for your well-being. Modeling that truth, however, takes much more than lip service and playacting. You can't just come home one evening and exclaim: "Boy, do I *love* my job! Work is just *great!*" This is when your kids' built-in baloney detectors start beeping at full volume, accompanied, of course, by rolled eyes.

Rather than try to whip up a load of false enthusiasm, you need to discover what you truly enjoy about your work. Almost every job—even a good job—involves a combination of things you enjoy, elements you simply put up with, and a few tasks you can barely stand. Most of life is like that. I love my cat, Stormy, and enjoy his company and his playfulness. For the sake of that, I put up with his miserable lack of tidiness around his litter box. But when I mention him to others, it's usually his positive qualities that I bring up.

Because we live in a largely negative society, it's easy to make every mention of our jobs negative, even if we really like our jobs. We're required to work too many hours, we deserve better pay, we're held to impossibly high standards. Grousing about one's job is the norm. And when something good is mentioned, it's usually related to compensation, not the work itself. "It's a great job—full benefits, a fully funded 401(k) plan, and stock options down the road!" But how often do we hear "It's a great job—full of challenging tasks, interesting coworkers, and significant results"? It's too bad we think only of compensation and so seldom of job satisfaction.

The ideal job is one that provides satisfying work while meeting your family's financial needs. If you're fortunate enough to have this, come home at night and express joy in projects accomplished, trucks loaded, or new products designed. When tempted to say something negative about your job around your children, bite your tongue. If you can't keep from mentioning a negative aspect of your work, make it clear that the benefits of working far outweigh the few disadvantages. "I can't stand the way my boss runs my division, but I still get to..." and fill in the blank with what keeps you coming back.

Is all this vigilance really needed? Believe me, there's no way your kids are going to value work if you don't. And if you value the wrong things about your job—the money, the recognition, and the prestige—your kids will pick that up as well. One reason why the man-in-the-gray-flannel-suit stereotype of the 1950s was so despised by the sixties generation was that he saw himself as an "organization man," an anonymous cog in a big machine. He lacked authenticity and real significance. He had exchanged his soul for a paycheck.

The opposite of being a nameless cog in the corporate machine is to exercise your soul through your work. You can redeem work from the realm of fallenness by approaching it not under the curse of Adam but as the creative endeavor that God designed it to be. When we value work as God's gift, it's likely that our children will catch the concept. Think of the outcome if they don't. There's something tragic about a twenty-something child who has yet to hold down a real job—especially if the parents are the ones still paying the bills.

Kids need to learn the importance of work early in life, and in the next chapter we'll look at how the home environment can serve as a laboratory for work attitudes that will last a lifetime. Or at least long enough for the kids to get paying jobs as ice-cream tasters, roller-coaster testers, or surfboard designers. Hey, *somebody* has to do it!

Chapter 6

A Wealth of Chores

Why Everyone Needs to Pitch In

Ryan was the child John and Nancy Wilson thought they'd never have. After years of prayer, fertility testing, and hoping, the Wilsons had given up. That's when Ryan came along. His parents had started late, and because they'd been successful in business they were able to provide their son with everything he wanted.

Ryan was loved by his nanny, who picked up his toys, made his bed, and cleaned and put away his clothes. He marveled at the horticultural skill of the yard crew that kept the Wilsons' landscaped acreage groomed with precision and elegance. Because Ryan's mother had been asthmatic as a child, she ensured that the housekeepers kept their home spotless. Even the cook took a special interest in Ryan, making him his favorite breakfast (pigs in a blanket) on the slightest pretext. He went to the best schools and took tennis and golf lessons—but nothing dangerous like football or wrestling, despite his larger-than-average size.

Today Ryan towers over his father's six-foot frame. He could easily pick up his mother and carry her around. He's also a bright young man. The thesis he wrote for his master's degree in political science was even published by an obscure academic press. Despite his obvious intelligence and talent, however, Ryan still hasn't found his place in life.

"What a shame that he's never found a job that suited him." That's how Nancy analyzed the jobless circumstances of her thirty-five-year-old son. These days, Ryan's chief occupations are golf, skiing, dating, and daytime television.

How could two highly successful people such as John and Nancy have raised such an unmotivated loafer? Unfortunately, the success that fueled their affluence also contributed to the forces that shaped their son into a well-educated and gifted loser. The Wilsons' wealth made it possible for family members to avoid the very thing that helps children acquire a healthy appreciation for work. John and Nancy hired away virtually every opportunity they had for training Ryan in the importance and dignity of labor. Ryan wasn't stupid; he understood that if his parents avoided chores around the house, then labor must be bad, or at least unnecessary.

Anyone who has read Laura Ingalls Wilder's Little House on the Prairie series or Mark Twain's *Tom Sawyer* knows that chores were a fact of life for most nineteenth-century children. Household tasks serve as a child's introduction to work and are one of the single most important tools for helping children develop marketable skills and the disciplines of diligence, pride of workmanship, personal responsibility, and conscientiousness. The home is the ideal environment for transmitting healthy attitudes about work and the significance of individuals contributing to the common good. The old-fashioned idea of sharing chores around the house gives parents the perfect opportunity to model an appreciative attitude toward work in front of their kids.

WHY CHORES MATTER

Attitudes are formed early in life. That's why chores—the unpaid labor performed by family members—should be introduced at a young age. Even in the nursery toddlers can learn that there are periodic (daily, weekly) pick-up times in which everyone helps put away the toys. As our kids grow, their responsibilities should increase. As we teach our kids the value of work and the pride of workmanship, there are three key principles to keep in mind.

Parents Pitch In

Our daughter, Laurie, took naturally to the tasks of putting away her toys and making her bed. But when Josh got big enough to clean his room, he would stand in the middle of the toy-strewn floor absolutely paralyzed by the magnitude of the job. He would work joyfully in partnership with me, but his motivation evaporated when I'd tell him, "Finish up, and I'll be back later to check on your progress."

Josh wasn't unusual in that regard. Many children joyfully attack their chores when the task masquerades as a family activity. Only a few children will stick with solitary jobs until they're completed. But especially with younger children, you'll get more results by taking a whole-family approach to chores.

My father had a gift for making any sort of work seem interesting. Even throughout the long, steamy summers, I could maintain a positive attitude toward yard work whenever my father was involved. Although he worked fast and hard, he never gave the impression that the work was drudgery. "Isn't this great!" was communicated not only by his broad grin but also by the effort he put into every aspect of the job.

Parents Lead the Celebration

We should always celebrate work and focus on the positive results that come from a job well done. After chore time, make it a family ritual to go from job to job as a group and express admiration and appreciation for a job well done. We're never too old to enjoy being appreciated for our efforts.

When I was growing up, every job ended with a time of appreciation and celebration. Even if we were only cleaning out the garage there would come a time when we'd stop and look around with satisfaction. Dad would say something like, "Look at all this room we have now! Maybe we should build a workbench in that corner where you could work on your model airplanes." Then we'd treat ourselves—sometimes only a cold shower followed by a 7UP in a glass jammed with crushed ice.

The combination of these crucial elements—parents pitching in and then leading the celebration—says clearly to your children: "Work is important, and your contribution is significant." Contrast this with a curt "Clean the basement!" followed by an unappreciative critique ("You didn't sweep in the corners!"). Sure, the basement might get cleaned (yeah, right!), but the experience has zero chance of building appreciation for that particular job or for work in general.

Parents Stress the Importance of Work

While parental involvement is essential, it's not necessary for every chore to become a team project. Once we've shown our kids how to perform a chore, it's practical to assign individual responsibilities. In fact, this progression becomes more important as our kids grow older. Household chores produce much more than simply an orderly home and a well-tended lawn. They present vivid examples of what happens when someone falls down on the job. In this regard, family pets provide an excellent training ground.

How many of you have heard, "Mommy! Can we *please* buy that puppy? I'll feed him and clean up after him!" If you've given in and bought a puppy (or kitten or hamster or parakeet), you've got a great opportunity to reinforce the idea that work is important and that failure to perform our assigned tasks produces serious consequences. If Justin fails to feed and water Barky or Tabby, the pet will die. And if he fails to take Barky outside, well, that just creates another round of unpleasant chores.

With pets, lessons are just waiting to be learned. So don't sidetrack the process by rescuing your kids when they grow bored and abdicate their pet-related chores, especially those deemed "gross" and "icky." Assign the jobs associated with Barky or Tabby along with appropriate consequences that will come into play if the child shirks his responsibilities. For example, nine-year-old Justin should be able to manage giving the dog food and clean water every day. When he forgets, the dog suffers. To avoid having a dead dog on your hands, you'll step in and feed and water Barky. But when the dog suffers, so should little Justin.

"Justin," you might say, "Barky needs his food and clean water every morning! What can we do so you'll remember to do it?" Brainstorm together to come up with systems that will help the dog get fed. If Justin has grown bored with his dog-feeding chores, that's the time to make clear that some jobs can't be avoided. Then make the consequences clear. "If you forget, I'll go ahead and feed Barky—but you'll lose TV privileges this weekend." And then follow through—no matter what!

Even wealthy families should ensure that they haven't engineered all opportunities for work out of their lives. If you have a lawn service, you can still reserve the weeding of flower beds for the family. If you have household help, schedule chores for the intervals between visits from cleaning professionals.

When you take advantage of the opportunities offered by household chores, you're training your children in many key attitudes regarding work. They'll learn from you that work is worth doing (because you're involved in it yourself), that their work is appreciated (because you lead the celebration when chores are completed), and that not doing key jobs leads to serious consequences (Barky collapses from hunger). The welfare of the family and the smooth operation of the home are dependent on every family member—including the children—doing his or her part.

Household chores are the kindergarten in the school of work. Failure at this level might not necessarily doom your children to become aimless, unemployed thirty-somethings who live at home while they watch ESPN and eat potato chips, but why plan to fail?

In the next chapter we'll look at the second aspect of Ryan-proofing your children: their first paying job. Should it be a lemonade stand or a newspaper route? No matter what the job, we need to look at the pros and cons of letting our kids work for money.

Chapter 7

Baby-Sitting and Lawn Care

Your Child's Home-Based Business Ventures

For many of his teenage years, my son, Josh, was the designated lawn-care technician in our family. In exchange for taking on this job, he sidestepped more than a few duties that he viewed as far more onerous and even unsanitary—the despised toilet cleaning, for example. Still, I recall the jaw-dropping experience of driving home and seeing Josh cheerfully pushing our lawn mower down the street. He was carrying a collection of garden tools that I would have bet were a greater mystery to him than the backside of the moon. Most shocking of all was the look of expectation on his headphone-draped face as he trudged down the sidewalk, bound I knew not where.

The mystery soon was solved. Some neighbors had hired my son to cut their grass. They were a group of single women, some of whom Kathy and I knew well enough that we could discreetly inquire about what kind of job Josh was doing. "Not bad at all," was the unanimous reply. Josh's customers were delighted with his work, and we were delighted that Josh had finally found a source of income.

Our daughter, Laurie, by contrast, was an old hand at making money. She was offered baby-sitting jobs at an early age, but for some odd reason she spurned anything connected with that line of work. Instead, she really enjoyed helping Kathy and me produce our monthly newsletter. Laurie soon learned how to streamline the process of folding, stuffing, labeling, and stamping more than three hundred newsletters.

Kathy and I could hardly believe our luck. Soon some of our Campus Crusade friends found out about Laurie's skills and hired her to do the same thing for them. In a few months our daughter had as many customers as she could handle. By then she had expanded her operations to include maintaining her clients' mailing lists on the family computer. In those days, such a skill seemed almost magical for adults, let alone a twelve-year-old.

THE VALUE OF PAID WORK

Laurie and Josh sought out their first jobs because they wanted more than the meager allowance (their assessment, not mine) that Kathy and I gave them. Throughout history, even young children helped support their families through their labor. In these more affluent times, most families can pay the bills without Justin's having to hire out his services. So is there any real benefit in encouraging our kids to pursue home-based work such as baby-sitting, doing lawn care, or cleaning houses for neighbors? (We'll consider more formal employment options in the following chapter.)

Remember that our initial goal is to help our children learn to appreciate work. The household chores discussed in chapter 6 introduce children to the beneficial aspects of work, teaching them that work must be taken seriously whether or not it is done for pay. As children grow older, however, they need to know that their labor has value, and exchanging their efforts for money is an important aspect of their training.

Both Laurie and Josh initiated their respective money-earning opportunities with very little understanding of the value of their labor. In fact, they both began on a "whatever you want to pay me" basis. In a short while, however, they had begun to analyze the value of their labor. Josh found out what other kids were paid for similar lawn jobs, and Laurie discovered what commercial services charged for mailing-service jobs. They began to learn that their labor had value, and they started evaluating what kind of bargain they could strike in exchange for their services. What pulled Josh, whistling as he trundled off with the lawn mower, was the lure of wages. He'd have spending money at last! Laurie, too, wanted those wages, but she was much more interested in the future opportunities her earnings would provide—so she typically saved most of her pay.

In addition to earning money—something they never received for doing family chores—they found themselves subjected to a new level of supervision. Working for others meant the kids couldn't use the old tricks that sometimes allowed substandard work to slide by at home. Their paymasters had a critical eye, and all the work had to meet an agreed-upon standard before any greenbacks were laid on the eagerly outstretched palms of my children.

So far these enterprises seemed a solid win-win situation: The kids earned their own money; their parents paid for fewer of the kids' expenses; the young workers began to explore the world of adult labor under the watchful eye of their neighbors and close family friends. But not every aspect of this situation was rosy.

KILLING SNAKES

When kids start working for money, there are three snakes in the grass that can blight this otherwise Edenic experience. We do ourselves, as well as our kids, a big favor when we're aware of the lurking reptiles. These threats to a successful home-based work experience are (1) the awareness of the value of their labor, (2) the temptation to work too much, and (3) parents who rescue their kids. Let's kill these snakes one by one.

The Value of Labor

The first snake that slithers into a child's home-based work world is his or her dawning awareness of the value of labor. When the child realizes that others will pay him or her for the same thing they do at home, they often decide that their parents ought to ante up as well. "Cut the grass? Sure, that'll be fifteen dollars, Dad." Parents need to draw a very clear line here. The fact that family members hold paying jobs outside the home does not mean that their contribution at home is now a fee-based service. Family chores, by definition, constitute unpaid labor.

"But I get ten dollars for mowing Mrs. Mulaney's lawn, and our yard is a lot bigger than hers!" This argument doesn't hold water. First, Mrs. Mulaney isn't a member of our family. She's a widowed septuagenarian who needs help with yard work. In contrast, our own lawn is enjoyed by our family, and the smooth operation of our household requires that it be mowed. Nobody pays parents for fixing meals, washing clothes, filing tax returns, or shopping for groceries. Likewise, children have the opportunity to participate in the family, and their occasional contribution includes whatever labor is appropriate.

I'm not saying that dealing with this issue is painless or stress-free, and if you're wise you'll work extra hard to make sure that family chores are done in a participatory and celebrative way. When your son washes the family car, make sure he gets his full share of praise and attaboys.

Working Too Much

Another serpent in the thicket of paid labor is that the young worker sometimes gets so enthused with this magical ability to make money that it begins to cut into other important aspects of life. Unless a family desperately needs the financial contributions of near-adult children, make sure your children's earning efforts remain a minor aspect of their lives.

How should we evaluate the priority of our children's jobs? If they expand to the point that sports, studies, or church activities are affected, it's time to set limits. I've known only a couple of children who've been so captivated by their earning ability that their parents had to rein them in. Both became wildly successful adults, but we don't want children to trade away the benefits of each stage of life for a comparatively small amount of money, especially money that they could easily earn later in life.

Parents' Rescue Attempts

The third snake that often shows up is the temptation for parents to step in to rescue their kids from their poor decisions. Your parental instinct is to make things easier for your children. In this case, ignore that instinct! This is a really good opportunity for your progeny to learn valuable lessons in the school of hard knocks.

A kid's newspaper route is a perfect example. The big brother of one of my childhood chums got a paper route. For several weeks he rode his bicycle all over the neighborhood flinging papers under cars, into bushes, and sometimes skipping our house entirely. Then the papers began to appear not only perfectly centered on the front walk but properly wrapped if there was even the slightest possibility of rain.

You guessed it—the kid's lax performance of his job had driven his well-meaning parents to take drastic action. Fearing for *their* reputation, this boy's parents took turns driving their young entrepreneur around the neighborhood and supervising his delivery methods. After a few weeks, their son lost interest in the job entirely. He remained in bed every morning while his parents finished out the remaining term of his job.

These parents didn't do their son any favors. He agreed to perform a demanding job and needed to learn how to carry out that job. But when his parents rushed in to rescue him, he was allowed to wriggle out of his responsibility. Unless there is a threat to your child's health or safety, you shouldn't bail out an unmotivated worker. We don't want our kids to accept any job thinking that if they lose interest their parents will take over. It doesn't work that way in the adult workplace, and our children need to learn that lesson now, while we're around to provide a safety net. Not being able to land a newspaper on a driveway from a moving bicycle is not sufficient reason to stay in bed while your parents do your job for you.

I'm not saying we shouldn't do what we can to help our children become conscientious, responsible workers. I admit I occasionally checked up on Josh's freshly mowed lawns, but the extent of my interference was to discreetly call his employers and plead with them to hold his work to the highest standards.

All in all, the tradition of children's earning a few bucks through home-based employment is a great transition from the world of unpaid chores to the wide world of part-time work outside the home. They begin to get a sense of the value of their labor, they have their first experience with a demanding nonparental boss, and they have the joy of acquiring money that hasn't first passed through the hands of mom or dad.

For some, this phase only whets their appetite for the next step—a real job outside the home with regular hours and an actual paycheck. While a job like this can be a great opportunity for some kids, in the next chapter we'll look at what we can do to ensure that it doesn't dead-end our kids' economic potential.

Chapter 8

"But I Want a *Real* Job!"

When Your Child Becomes a Part-Time Employee

Mike and Heather were delighted when Jason snagged a summer job at the local Burger Quick after his third year in high school. What better way for him to learn the value of a dollar, they thought, than by working in that all-American sweatshop known as a fast-food franchise? They were less than pleased, though, when all of Jason's earnings magically disappeared into his CD collection, several nearly indistinguishable pairs of astronomically expensive sunglasses, and a year-round pass to a high-energy amusement park.

The glow really wore off when Jason kept his job after school started again in the fall. His grades started edging lower, and by spring his chances of getting into the college of his choice were reduced to two: slim and none. "That's all right," he cheerfully explained. "I've been accepted into management training at Burger Quick!"

We all want our children to value work and learn perseverance, industriousness, and other traits that will enable them to succeed in the adult work world. But we don't want them to get so hooked on working that it locks them out of the long-term options that they're still too young to grasp. Jason's college plans fell by the way-side when he started thinking about a career with Burger Quick. When our kids start to say, "But I want a *real* job," what can we do to help them keep their options for later life, especially college, open? A good place to start is by reaching an agreement—in writing.

THE JOB CONTRACT

Teenagers are old enough to make many of their own decisions, but there is a type of tether that will keep them connected to you. In this case it's a simple contract. You and your would-be wage earner need to sit down and hammer out a written agreement before he or she accepts an out-of-the-home job. It will eliminate buckets of conflict down the road and will put your offspring on notice that holding a job is a privilege that carries significant responsibilities. So as you write up your contract, make sure you spell out mutual agreements in the areas of safety, time require-ments, parental expectations, and disposal of income. Let's look at the four clauses in this contract.

Safety
You would obviously veto any job that would put your child's physical safety at risk, such as night cashier at a frequently robbed gas station. It's also important to spell out that no job is acceptable

if a safe manner of commuting to work can't be established. Since this job is to be your child's responsibility, don't get yourself into a situation where you have to drive your teen to or from his job unless it's already on your commuting route.

But physical safety isn't the only danger lurking in the world of part-time employment. Not long ago I was amazed to find a high schooler manning the counter at a convenience store that gave him (not to mention his customers) ready access to alcohol, tobacco, and pornographic magazines. What could his parents have been thinking when they said yes to that job?

Time Requirements
Some part-time jobs involve only a few hours per week, while others can absorb major chunks of your child's discretionary time. Most of the benefits of working outside the home can be met with a job that requires only eight to ten hours per week. After all, you want your child to have time for other important aspects of growing up, especially church, sports, and cultural involvement (music, art, theater).

Some kids easily become overinvolved in their jobs. Sometimes they have jobs with real responsibility, and they're treated more like adults at work than anywhere else. If they are under pressure to increase their hours or work extra shifts, it can be helpful for them to be able to tell their manager, "Sorry, my parents only allow me to work twelve hours each week."

Parental Expectations
A part-time job is usually a child's first experience with the demands of the working world, particularly such mundane re-

quirements as showing up on time and being properly groomed and dressed. Like most conscientious parents, you'll probably feel a near-overwhelming compulsion to "help" Justin wake up in time for his job at the Shake 'n' Bacon. As it becomes painfully evident that he is going to be late for his shift, you also notice that his uniform is artistically spattered with a rainbow of flavored-syrup stains.

Now is the time to get a grip on yourself. Refuse to shift into rescue mode. So what if Justin is late for work? Getting yelled at by his shift manager may be exactly what he needs to begin to develop the daily disciplines that will enable him to function in real-world work environments. And if he gets another dose of reality compliments of his syrup-spattered uniform, isn't that all to the good as well?

Most kids have been exposed since early childhood to well-intentioned parents droning, "If you don't get up *right now* you'll be late *again!*" and "Isn't that the same shirt you've worn *every day* this week?" As near-adults, they don't need to hear you deliver those messages—but they desperately need to experience for themselves the consequences of slacking off. But what if, brace yourself, your little darling gets fired? Don't despair—there are plenty of jobs out there, and the lessons a kid can learn from being fired are ones that only a nonparent can teach.

Make it clear in your job contract that your teen is responsible for getting to work on time (even if it means walking, riding a bicycle, or taking a bus), ensuring that his clothes are clean, and that you will not bail him out or make excuses to his boss. On the other hand, spell out exceptions to the general policies: "Justin will ride his bike to work unless it is raining," and so forth.

Use of Earnings

Most children who seek part-time employment are motivated by the lure of earning money. Having determined that their allowance (more on that later) is insufficient for their wants, they see a part-time job as an endless source of financial benefits. So don't wait until they cash their first paycheck before you establish expectations on how that money is to be spent. Make your job contract very specific on this point.

Three of your child-rearing goals are to help your offspring learn to save wisely, give generously, and spend carefully. A part-time job gives you and your child a chance to put those principles into practice, but they need to be spelled out in the contract.

For example, you could establish percentages for saving, giving, and spending from each paycheck. Since this is probably discretionary income, consider a breakdown that allows approximately 25 percent of the take-home pay to be spent any way that your child likes (assuming it's moral, legal, and doesn't pose a health or safety hazard). Agree on a suitable portion, perhaps 10 to 20 percent, to be given to the church and other charitable causes, and earmark the rest for savings. Depending on your family's financial situation, that could be long-term savings for college tuition or a future need beyond college, such as a more reliable car.

By spelling out these issues in advance—and many of them will require negotiation and compromise—you'll avoid a great deal of grief later. It will help your child understand some of the real responsibilities of holding a part-time job, and it will go a long way to promoting a positive first work experience.

ALTERNATIVES TO JOBS

Part-time jobs are not ideal for every kid. Some have special talents or abilities that really need to be developed, and traditional jobs for teenagers can interfere with that training. Sometimes the goals of a part-time job can be reached in other ways, especially through the discipline of team sports and other group activities.

Consider the seventeen-year-old who is the editor of her large high school's weekly student newspaper. It's unlikely that a part-time job could come close to teaching the technical and managerial skills of an unpaid job like that. Demanding team sports also can teach the same lessons learned in a part-time job. If you take into account the discipline of training, learning to play under the coach's direction, and forging working relationships with other teammates, there are few part-time jobs that would confer similar benefits.

Finally, not all jobs need to come with a paycheck. Most of the character benefits of a part-time job can also be found in well-supervised volunteer work. A weekly commitment to helping out at the local humane society could be better preparation for an aspiring veterinarian than pitching newspapers from a bicycle every morning. Volunteering at the local Y or youth club is likely to be better training for a would-be social worker than putting in ten hours as a fry cook at Lester's Roadside Diner. How could a would-be teacher find a better part-time job than volunteering as a reading tutor at the Head Start center?

In addition to the character benefits, another by-product of your child's working life will be the earnings that accompany it.

Kids need to learn early, even at the sandbox stage, that wealth of all kinds belongs to God, and that he has made us responsible to use it wisely. One of the most significant uses for the money that God puts into our hands is to pass it on. Most kids are naturally generous, but they all need an occasional shove in the right direction. In the next section we'll look at helping our kids learn the art of generous giving.

PART III

PRINCIPLE 2:
GIVE GENEROUSLY

Generosity Begins in the Sandbox

It's Never Too Early to Teach Openhandedness

A few years ago I revisited the very poor Asian country where my family lived when our children were growing up. This time I took my college-age son with me as my computer network assistant. We worked together at the seminary I'd helped start in 1982, trying to bring it into the Information Age.

I make frequent teaching trips to very poor countries, so the hardships of life in the Third World were fresh in my memory. But Josh had lived in the United States since we returned from Asia. He was eight years old then, so he had forgotten many of the scenes of human suffering that are common in the underdeveloped world.

Josh and I were seeing the same sights of misery, but my son was seeing them with fresh and caring eyes. To my surprise, I found that I'd become programmed to ignore the reaching hands of beggars and the heartbreaking countenances of hungry children to whom even a piece of chewing gum was a rare luxury. While I was concerned with not getting scammed and keeping our pockets from being picked, Josh was interested in what he could do to help these desperate people. I realized that even as a college student, he hadn't lost the generous spirit that often characterizes children.

Most young children are naturally openhanded. If you jokingly ask a toddler if you can share her sucker, she'll take it out of her mouth and try to stick it in yours. We might chuckle at such innocence, but I'm convinced that openhandedness is one of the most important of all human traits. I'm equally convinced that it was one of the most appealing aspects of Jesus' ministry. He received from his heavenly Father the power to heal, to feed the multitudes, and to forgive sins—and he did all those things without a hint of reluctance. He knew that he had full access to God's limitless resources, so why *not* be generous? The supply would never diminish, no matter how much Jesus gave away to the needy people who came to him.

As parents, a crucial part of our job is to build this same quality of generosity into our children. We want them to see material possessions not as the goal of living and not as prizes to be hoarded, but as gifts from a loving God. In turn, we are to enjoy these gifts in a loving relationship with both our heavenly Father and our earthly brothers and sisters.

If we fail to instill this value in our children, what will determine their attitude toward possessions? We need only look around us to see the values of a materially focused generation. A recent issue of *Wired* magazine highlighted the baubles of the hyper-rich: mechanical wristwatches for eighty thousand dollars, speedboats as big as a house, and private jets that cost eight figures. If young people view these things as legitimate goals in life, how likely are they to be openhanded with what they have?

A look around any college campus shows that the slogan from the eighties "The one who dies with the most toys wins!" is still alive and well. Many students spend their college savings on an endless stream of electronic toys. MP3 players and cell phones top the list, followed closely by absurdly expensive "personal accessories," typically overly styled sunglasses for guys and extremely pricey handbags for girls. Bear in mind that I'm not talking about the sons and daughters of rich parents. These are the average kids, the ones who fund their consumerism with credit cards. These students make up a growing segment of the staggering percentage who graduate from college with significant credit-card debt.

Understand that I'm not against cool sunglasses or MP3 players. It's not wrong for a student to own a cell phone or the latest PlayStation. The problem comes when the owner sees these possessions as essential components of a quality life. It's all a matter of perspective. The proper regard for material possessions is as an accent to life—the pepper and salt that season a joyful life already packed with good things. Material possessions can never define who and what we are. We find our true identity as sons and daughters of God, not as owners of a nearly new BMW.

Almost three thousand years ago one of the richest men in history, King Solomon, described the emptiness of a life that exists in isolation from God. Solomon's reflections on this state are recorded in the Old Testament book of Ecclesiastes.[1] He advised his readers to enjoy the material things of life, accepting them as the gracious gifts of God, but also to understand that they can only be appreciated in the context of a joyous relationship with God (Ecclesiastes 2:24-25).

How do we begin to inculcate this mind-set into our children? Most kids are born possessing the conflicting extremes of open-handed generosity and grasping materialism. How many parents have been astounded when they ask their offspring, "Where's the new Game Boy your grandparents gave you for Christmas?" and heard, "Oh, I let Tyler borrow it. He lost his." We hope Tyler doesn't lose this one, too, but we're thrilled that our child exhibited such generosity. The irony is that this same child can readily demonstrate the opposite approach to possessions, dissolving into a screaming paroxysm of "It's mine, *mine*, MINE!" when asked to share one of his treasured toys.

REINFORCING GENEROSITY

Given this paradoxical childhood bent toward both sharing and selfishness, parents need to place a high priority on cultivating a spirit of generosity. We need to be proactive, offering positive rein-forcement whenever we see openhanded behavior.

When I've watched toddlers playing together in a sandbox, I've seen examples of pure sharing: Toys are handed back and forth without clinging, crying, or complaining. That's the moment when a wise parent springs into action with a flood of approval, including verbal praise and hugs. Another way to reinforce openhandedness is to downplay the chances of your child's toy being lost or broken. If a child fears that her treasured doll will lose an arm, she'll be less likely to let a friend play with it. Since most children need to ele-vate their generosity quotient, you should make the most of every opportunity. "Mommy, we're getting ice cream?" "Yes, Justin. I saw how you shared your action figures with those other boys."

Constructive reinforcement is preferable to punishment. Don't switch tactics in midstream. "Mommy, you said we were getting ice cream!" "Well, Justin, that was before you refused to share your Legos with your sister!" Such a reversal will lead to an unhappy experience for both child and parent, and what lesson is learned? "So, first my sister tries to take all my Legos and now it's *her* fault that I don't get ice cream!" Stick with reinforcing the positive attitudes you observe.

Using positive reinforcement to train our children is in line with the example of Jesus (see Matthew 7:9-11). The goal is to create positive attitudes toward sharing, giving, and letting go. Positive attitudes are built through praise and affirmation, not through the pain of being punished.

Be proactive in helping your young children succeed in the area of sharing. Put your toddlers in supervised play situations that will reinforce the virtue of openhandedness. Explain to other parents that you're encouraging generosity, and make sure that play dates are not just recreational, but that they will also provide opportunities for learning lessons in character.

As you set up opportunities for learning, work out a consistent routine for dealing with grabby and nonsharing children. When your child is a victim of another child's selfish behavior, try to make a helpful point without being excessively negative. "Jennifer, I can understand how upset you must feel. What should Kaitlyn have done instead?" By discussing what *should* have been done, instead of concentrating on Kaitlyn's stinginess, you are helping your child picture a higher standard of behavior.

But let's say *your* child is the one being selfish! You may be wondering if there isn't an appropriate place for negative reinforcement in training your child in his first steps toward learning the joy of giving. There are two steps you can take to address a young child's stinginess. At the moment of a child's unwillingness to share, you can issue a warning: "Justin, remember that toys are for sharing. Let Megan play with the truck." If Justin persists in hogging the toy, you can warn him again—but this time use a time-out.

Later, you can reinforce the lesson in a more positive way. Let's say you and Justin are watching a nature show on TV. A pride of lions is feasting on a delicious, freshly killed wildebeest. They are crowding each other to get to the tastiest parts. You could use this as a learning moment. "Look, Justin, that smaller lion isn't being allowed to get any food!" You can then discuss the fact that animals typically are concerned about themselves without regard for others, while God created people to care for the needs of others.

THE NEXT STAGE

No one wants to picture his or her sweet, wobbly little toddler ever growing up to become a greedy, uncaring, money-grabbing adult. We don't want our delightful, gifted kids to ever base their self-worth on the car they drive or the neighborhood they move into. That's why we need to recognize the long-term effects of how we train our children. We should take steps to help mold the character qualities into our kids now that we want them to demonstrate as they grow up.

Lessons learned when your child is young will become deeply

rooted. Beware, however, of regarding your child as a kind of human bonsai, capable of being shaped to any form merely by exercising your will. Your children will make many choices on the way to independent adulthood, and most of those choices will be made without your involvement. (If you have more than one child, you already know that some kids are less easily influenced by their parents.)

But a foundation laid in these early years will prepare your young children with the building blocks of a good character just in time for the next stage, when they are able to think through their actions and make their own decisions. Remember, your long-term goal is to produce independent adults who will be internally motivated to give generously, save wisely, spend carefully, and avoid financial disasters. Even though little Justin doesn't even know his numbers yet, he knows "mine!" And even at the sandbox stage it's not too early for him to understand the joys of unclenching that tightly gripped fist.

In a few years you may watch your child acting independently on the character you're struggling to help develop in these early years. My family moved back to the United States in 1986 from Asia, where we had seen plenty of news coverage of America's homeless problem. I had taken Josh, then about eight, with me to run some errands downtown, and as we stood at a red light, out of the corner of my eye I noted and dismissed a homeless man sitting on the sidewalk nearby. He wore disheveled clothes, had long, matted hair, and held a badly lettered sign reading "Vietnam Vet— Please Help."

The crossing light turned green, and I looked around for Josh. That's when I saw my eight-year-old putting money into the hands of a panhandler. I had to struggle with my emotions—shame that I had no compassion for this impoverished person blended with irritation that Josh's gift (half of his allowance) would probably be used to buy cheap wine. What finally dawned on me as Josh caught up and we crossed the street together was a sense of a job well begun.

Had Josh wasted his allowance? Was his gift a wise decision? That's not the right question to ask. What matters is that a young boy saw life through generous eyes. He was openhanded. Life to Josh was more than how much candy that money would buy, and I exulted in this sign of his developing character.

Looking beyond the toddler stage to children who can think through their actions and make their own decisions, we can introduce the concept of giving in a more formal way. God owns everything, and he loans us some of his material possessions. So when we give something away, we're only giving God's wealth, and we can't possibly diminish the supply. In the next chapter we'll look at some practical first steps toward systematic giving and learn how to inculcate a taste for generous giving in our budding young philanthropists.

Chapter 10

Teaching Joyful Giving

Adding a Smile to Openhandedness

My family played on the beach one afternoon while I went snorkeling in the South China Sea. Through my goggles I noticed an old tuna can on the bottom of the ocean. Swimming down to retrieve it, I was baffled to find a sand dollar stuck tight to its opening. A mysterious unseen force resisted my efforts to pull the sand dollar off the open end of the can. What was holding on so tightly from inside? It turned out the tuna can was the home of an octopus.

I swam back to the beach, shouting at the kids to come and look. The octopus, however, began to push on the sand dollar that served as the door to his home—and he could really shove, considering he weighed less than a pound! With all my strength I couldn't prevent him from forcing the sand dollar off that tin can, and his escape became inevitable.

Attempting to outwit the octopus, I suddenly released my pressure on his lid. Sensing a trick, he immediately slammed shut again. I reinforced his sense of insecurity by periodically pulling at his sand dollar as though it were my greatest wish to open it and get him out.

My reverse psychology worked, and my wide-eyed kids soon gathered to stare at the dripping tuna can. "What is it, Papa? What's in there?"

"You'll see," I answered, and in a few minutes they ran shrieking as my hapless captive erupted from his can and teetered terrifyingly on tentacle tips before flopping around on the picnic table.

I soon returned him (and his home) to the safety of the reef, but my children never forgot their encounter with a live, canned octopus. The flailing tentacles impressed them, and I learned a lesson that I often applied with my kids as they grew older. I call it the Octopus Principle. It simply means that once you decide what character quality you want your kids to develop, make it easy for them to acquire it. Sometimes that means holding them back, but it can also mean pushing them along. And when it comes to generosity, children are usually easily pushed in the right direction.

As your children move from the toddler and preschool stage to elementary school age, they still are likely to demonstrate surprising acts of generosity. Whenever you notice one, cherish and affirm this behavior. Even as they are learning addition and subtraction, they should be encouraged to develop good attitudes toward giving.

The principles of Christian giving are so basic even a child can grasp them. The starting point is the recognition that God owns everything: the universe, us, and every single item that we think of as being "ours." Whether we've inherited our money, sweated for it on the assembly line, or had it dropped in our lap through a lucky investment, it's still God's money that he has entrusted to us. The challenge for us, and the goal to which we're raising our children, is to manage well what God has loaned us.

Giving is the starting point in a Christian approach to money management because it constantly reminds us who *really* owns the assets. Children have a head start in this area, because as far as they are concerned, all of their assets (toys, candy, comics, Pokémon cards, PlayStations, clothes, books, and so on) flow mysteriously from a higher power—their parents. Just as Jesus' generosity was based on the fact that he was distributing the assets of his limitlessly wealthy heavenly Father (see Psalm 50:10-11), so kids can be encouraged to be generous with the assets of their earthly parents. In other words, take steps to channel some of your giving through the hands of your children.

I'm not talking about giving each of the kids a dollar to put in the church collection plate. I'm suggesting that they be brought into family giving strategies as junior partners. In order to prepare them for that stage, which I'll cover more thoroughly in the next chapter, they need to begin to give in ways that are appropriate for younger children.

THREE CRUCIAL GIVING ATTITUDES

We want our kids to establish a lifestyle of giving that will continue in their adult years. To help ground them in an openhanded approach to life, we need to help them develop certain attitudes toward their possessions and sharing what they have.

First, they need to see themselves as wealthy in comparison with others who have not been so financially blessed. Our children need to know that God has given to them abundantly, and that

God can use them—even at a young age—to give to others who have greater needs.

Many parents, on reading this, might react by saying, "But we're not wealthy!" Let's talk honestly for a minute. If you can afford to buy a book like this one (or even meet the minimum requirements to get a library card), you are in the wealthiest 25 percent of the earth's population. If your life is a constant parade of financial crises and you're always struggling to make ends meet, it's probably not an income problem. More money won't solve most financial problems, but wise financial management will.

You're in a perfect position to model the truth that a loving God meets the financial and physical needs of your family, and that he also enables you to help meet the needs of others. To demonstrate that in front of your children, you need to live on less than you earn so the difference between revenues and expenditures will be available for wise saving and generous giving. Taking stock of the needs of others is a great way to acknowledge God's blessings in our lives. We truly are wealthy.

Second, kids need an abiding sense of security. They need to feel secure in their parents' love, and as they grow older they should know that their financial security is rooted in God's care for them. Whether your family is experiencing an economic boom or bust, make sure you honor God for meeting your needs. Cultivate a sense of thankfulness and gratitude that your present needs are met rather than constantly sending up a series of "we need more everything!" prayers.

Third, if your kids are convinced that God meets your family's needs, then they can be generous in their giving. That means you need to decide where and how to give. The church is an obvious starting point, but children often find the traditional "quarter in the offering plate" a somewhat baffling ritual. The money goes into the plate, is carried out of the church sanctuary, and then disappears. It is much easier for them to visualize what takes place when the church is collecting canned goods for the local food kitchen.

LIFESTYLE LESSONS

Many of today's middle-class children grow up without ever coming into contact with people who really *don't* have enough to eat or a place to sleep or warm clothes to wear. Most middle-class kids attend school with other middle-class kids and go to churches where everybody comes from the same homogenous segment of society. They need to learn what life is like outside their particular tuna can.

We do our children a huge favor when we introduce them early on to a much broader cross-section of the human family. Many parents believe that a cross-cultural missions trip as a teenager is the best time to make this introduction. I disagree. By that time a child has already defined a "normal" standard of living, typically one that is biased toward materialism and consumption. So take steps to introduce your young children to segments of the community that are disadvantaged. Even preschoolers can benefit from opportunities to experience life at different economic scales.

When children understand that God shares his wealth with us, and that we are to imitate him by sharing with others, they can start to think about specific ways to give. Encourage your children to give some of their allowance or a few of their toys to help meet the needs of others. It may be a church offering, a missions project, or the local homeless shelter. Every time you pass a Salvation Army kettle at Christmas, make sure each of your kids drops in a generous gift.

As they learn that a heavenly Father meets the needs of their own family, they know they can give from the abundance that they've received. But how do they know that they've received abundantly? Through systematic exposure to a lower economic stratum. And where do they get the assets to give abundantly? From their earthly parents, who received them from that same heavenly Father. It doesn't matter that they are giving away money from *your* billfold. The important thing is that they are learning the principle of giving away what God has entrusted to them.

Don't worry that your children will become too generous. Sometimes children will want to give unwisely, as in giving panhandlers money that might be spent on alcohol or drugs. Discernment in giving will be an important lesson they can learn later on, but for now the key is to encourage them to acquire the habit of giving to meet the needs of others. Our culture is so me-focused that even kids with the most generous spirits will face an uphill battle to hang on to a generous attitude. Take advantage of their most teachable years by going out of your way to encourage generous giving.

At every age, do what you must to help your kids see the world outside of their own particular tuna can. Remember the Octopus Principle. Once you decide what character quality you want your kids to develop, make it easy for them to develop it. Some kids will need holding back, but most will benefit from a gentle push to move them in the right direction. As young children, they can begin to acquire the giving attitudes that will help them resist the siren call of materialism and consumerism.

As you teach your children about openhandedness, be aware that the teenage years are particularly crucial. In the next chapter we'll examine how an allowance can lay the foundation for a more adult approach to giving.

Chapter 11

The Lesson of Allowances

A Little Cash Can Be the Key to Independent Giving

"You don't pay a cent—this offer is *FREE!*" At my age, I should know better. But I'm still a sucker for that little four-letter word.

The promise of getting something free scratches an itch deep within our human nature. One of the reasons for the ongoing popularity of government-sponsored giveaway programs is the notion that someone else winds up paying for what we get. But in real life, as a sage using imperfect grammar once said, "There ain't no free lunch." Or is there?

There is one sense in which we all have access to a free lunch, and everything that goes with it. God gives to us freely of life, time, friends, family, the spiritual blessings of being a part of God's family—I could go on and on. As we seek to raise kids who will manage their money wisely, we need to help them understand that all wealth ultimately flows from God. It's a great privilege to pass these riches on to others in need.

When children are young, we parents start to establish the habit of giving by having them give something that is actually ours. But as they grow older, it's important that kids start to give away a portion of the money they consider their own. That's what makes an allowance one of the best tools to help children learn not only the value of money, but also the wonder of giving it away.

An allowance, given the right emphasis, can divert our kids' focus from "What will I buy?" to "How can I help?" An allowance is a child's first opportunity to establish money-management patterns that can influence his or her adult life. Let's look at how we can turn the time-honored tradition of a kid's allowance into a tool for shaping our children's character.

PAYMENT OR GIFT?

In an earlier chapter on helping children appreciate work, I mentioned that an allowance should not be given as a payment for doing household chores. Parents aren't paid for cooking, ironing, and running a taxi service. Likewise, kids need to do their part, without the expectation of being paid, to keep the home running smoothly. Here are four reasons why it's a bad idea to connect your child's allowance with household chores.

First, it sends the wrong message. Paying for chores connects the concepts of "work" and "pay" too closely in your children's minds. Work should not be seen primarily as a way to generate cash. It should be viewed as a higher and nobler task. God created us to be co-creators with him, so work is worth doing—and doing well—even if it doesn't earn a wage.

Second, it leads to other problems down the road. If you start paying your kids to do chores, then every request for help ("Justin, it's time to feed the dog") is likely to turn into a labor negotiation ("How much do I get if I do?"). Well, Justin gets a comfortable home to live in, clothes, food, an education, and recreational outlets—all at no cost to him. In turn, he has a responsibility to share the workload within the family. When everyone shares the labor, everyone succeeds.

Third, linking allowances and household chores will backfire if your kids are unmotivated. When I was a kid, if I'd had a choice between doing chores or doing without money, I would probably have chosen the latter. Kids who would settle for no allowance would miss out on the key money management lessons you want to teach them. You can't learn to play Monopoly without having access to Monopoly money. Likewise, learning to manage money requires access to actual money. Keeping allowances separate from household labor provides a ready supply of cash to help your children learn the ABCs of money management.

Fourth, paying your children for doing chores makes it harder for them to give money away. If your children had to work for every cent they own, they might become excessively attached to their money. But by giving them an allowance that is independent of their performance of household chores, you make it easier for them to do the right thing—give freely to others.

MONITOR THE ALLOWANCE

Once you decide to give your kids an allowance, you need to settle on an amount and then determine how much control you'll exercise over what your kids do with the money. The short answer to the amount question is "never give them enough." The quick answer to the parental control question is "lots of control!"

When determining an appropriate amount for an allowance, never give your kids enough money so that they can immediately satisfy their current needs—or their desires, whims, and cravings. If you do, you'll rob them of the lessons of deferring gratification, saving, and careful spending. If you give them too much allowance, they won't have to determine which of two conflicting options (movie tickets or a music CD) is the best use of their money. When money is limited, it forces a child to carefully think through the issues of saving, giving, and wise spending.

When it comes to parental control, part of the purpose of an allowance is to teach your kids the basics of wise money management. As such, you need to exert appropriate control over what they do with their money. While parents reserve final veto authority over how their kids use their money, it's possible to encourage your children to give from their allowance without exercising *undue* control. You want your kids to develop internal motivations for saving, giving, and careful spending—not simply knuckle under to your manipulation.

The earlier you start, the easier it will be for your children to establish good patterns. Allowances should begin when a child is four or five. It needn't be much money—a few quarters a week is enough to get started. Once you begin the allowance, be on the lookout for opportunities to train your kids in wise saving, giving, and spending. Notice when they demonstrate a built-in motivation to give something. It may be something very concrete—they saw a homeless person sleeping in a doorway or an advertisement for a charity seeking to feed hungry children in the Third World. That's the time to explain to Justin that he is old enough to be deciding how he will use his allowance money each week. It's up to him to decide how to use it within the boundaries of two important restrictions: He *must* give some, and he *must* save some. Explain that some of it must be saved for future needs (covered in a later chapter), and some of it should be made available to give to people in need, like that homeless person or hungry child.

MAKE GIVING VISIBLE

Younger children respond readily to concrete examples. But since it's unlikely that there is a needy person right there in your home, I suggest you combine a lesson on giving with a craft project. You and your child can make a "giving jar" (you could also call it a "joy jar"—or not!) into which your child's money can be put until it is delivered to the appropriate charitable agency. Use a large jar so it can be covered with illustrations representing the kinds of needs that your child finds compelling.

The key here is to allow the child to develop a sense of what pushes her motivational buttons for giving. It's possible to have several different jars, each representing a different target for giving. One for a missionary, one for an adopted Third World child, and one for the local homeless shelter. When you give your child her allowance, make sure it's delivered as several smaller coins so she can divide it up. Instead of giving a quarter to a four-year-old, give twenty-five pennies, or possibly five nickels. The idea is to give the child a lot of flexibility in allocating her giving, saving, and spending.

Even when the child has put money in the giving jar, keep

repeating what a wise and gracious thing she has done. You can pray together that the gift will be used in a great way in helping to meet the needs of people. And remember, God takes little or no note of the actual size of a gift. It is very possible that children giving pennies make up the gifts that please God the most. Jesus used the lunch of one small boy to feed a hungry multitude.

Be aware of the short attention span of children, and make sure that the money put into the giving jar quickly finds its way to its destination. You may be tempted to empty the jar, quickly write a check, shove it in an envelope, and be done with it. Don't! It's important for children to see the money they put in the jar go to the recipient agency. If you take the change from the jar, put it in your pocket, and write out a check, it can confuse younger children. Best of all is to take the actual giving jar to the Salvation Army shelter and let your child personally hand the money to a worker. Of course, you can take advantage of the opportunity to add a donation of your own—without stealing any of your kid's thunder, of course.

This may sound like a lot of trouble for a very small amount of money. Don't be misled. For a small amount of money and a little trouble, you're buying a priceless education for your budding philanthropists. You're teaching your children that they can make significant gifts with their money. You're taking steps to ensure that allowances aren't immediately seen as "what can I buy for me!" occasions but as opportunities to help others.

Of course, learning to give joyfully, systematically, and strategically is only one of the goals of giving your children allowances. They'll also be trained in saving and spending skills. Even a small allowance at an early, impressionable age gives us a priceless chance to help mold our children's character. As they grow, allowances increase, possessions become more valuable, and they may actually, when they are teenagers, begin to earn their own money.

In the next chapter we'll study the thorny problem of helping increasingly independent children develop mature, adult patterns of giving. As usual, we parents must be willing to use our influence sparingly, yet effectively. And what does it cost us to shape our children's generous spirit? Absolutely nothing—it's *FREE!*

Chapter 12

The Teenage Philanthropist

Helping Your Adolescent Cultivate Generosity

For weeks during the summer of my eleventh year, I waited every day for the mailman. He was going to bring me a remote-control model submarine! I still remember the TV commercial, especially the sub's sleek gray lines and even the realistic pinging sounds emitted by an enemy destroyer as the sub made its underwater escape.

When the mailman finally made the delivery, I was absolutely horrified. The submarine was a molded toy only a few inches long—powered by baking soda! My disappointment over the sub, however, didn't prevent me from falling for an endless succession of sucker toys aimed at children.

How can marketers so easily manipulate children? One reason is that TV presents an idealized vision of a life that includes the adored object. In the commercials, life gets a lot better when the child on TV owns the desired toy. As parents, we can use this vision of a better future to our advantage. We can help our children picture a future in which other people lead better lives because our kids use their gifts to bring about significant change. As kids grow older, they really do possess the ability to make a difference for God's kingdom.

If your kids are teenagers or approaching adolescence, they may already be getting a sizable allowance. In addition, they may be earning money from occasional paid work or part-time jobs. Older children in the United States control billions of dollars of disposable income. Marketing campaigns aimed at teenagers present powerful evidence of the collective economic power of today's adolescents.

Since our kids' wealth increases with age, we need to keep the vision of significant giving before their eyes. They also need to discover a style of giving that will become a lifelong pattern of philanthropy. At this age, their giving can make a real impact in their own neighborhood, their community, and the world. When children see the difference their gifts make, they're often hooked on a lifetime of philanthropy.

When giving characterizes a person's life it dramatizes the biblical truth that we belong to God and that he not only owns us, but he owns all our possessions as well (see 1 Corinthians 6:19-20 and Psalm 24:1). Giving reinforces the fact that God is our ultimate source of love and security—for a lifetime.

Giving also produces some very practical life benefits. It helps head off a rampant selfishness that would otherwise lead to envy and lack of contentment. Our natural inclinations, if left unchecked, would drive us to devote our lives to fulfilling our own wants, desires, and cravings. A lifestyle of giving produces something far more satisfying. By helping our children cultivate an outward-looking, giving character, we're contributing to their fulfillment as adults.

A TEEN'S GIVING DECISIONS

As your children grow, it's not as easy to steer their giving. They want to make their own decisions, and you need to help them develop a frame of reference—a grid—through which to screen opportunities for giving. The key to encouraging a heart for giving is to bring them into the process of making family-based donations.

As my own children were growing up in Asia and later in Southern California, they had plenty of opportunities to see people in various kinds of financial need. In Asia they came to know many Christian workers, and Kathy and I frequently discussed in their presence our thought processes as we decided on whether to help finance a particular missionary or charitable relief project.

My children have different slants on what pushes their charitable buttons. Josh is much more attracted to agencies that help relieve physical suffering associated with poverty and disease, while Laurie is drawn to helping meet spiritual needs. As our children were growing to adulthood, we tried to provide opportunities for all kinds of giving and encouraged them to participate.

One fall we went to a poor suburb of Tijuana, Mexico, to help set up an open-air showing of the *Jesus* film. It had been some time since either of my kids had been in a Third World situation, but it was great to see how comfortable they were interacting with local children as they passed out fliers advertising the show. Afterward, I watched in amazement as Laurie worked her way through a simple Spanish presentation of the gospel with a Mexican woman who was intent on understanding the message of the booklet.

After that experience they were much more interested in our annual discussions about what aspect of the ministry of the *Jesus* film we wanted to help fund as a family. Should our gift be designated for translation, covering the expenses of traveling film teams, or providing heavy-duty projection equipment? After our trip to Tijuana, my kids could picture exactly how our family's gift would be used, and as a result they were intensely interested in our financial involvement in the project.

A few years ago we discovered Partners International, an agency that identifies effective Third World ministries and then provides financial and technical assistance. We received a wonderful "catalogue" from them showing how a given gift could translate into changed lives. For example, $4 could provide a hoe to a subsistence farmer in Ghana, and $450 would finance an eight-month pastoral training program for sixteen village pastors in Burma.

That October we met as a family around the kitchen table and each of us was given one-fourth of our total gift to allocate among the various opportunities described in the catalog. We had a great time deciding how each of us would distribute resources based on criteria such as urgency of need (Josh opted for water wells in Africa) or geographical interests (Laurie had a friend living in Nepal).

Family giving experiences can be an effective complement to family vision trips or even mission trips. You don't have to go to the Third World to introduce your children to great giving opportunities. Take the whole family to participate in helping prepare and serve a Thanksgiving or Christmas dinner at the local Salvation Army shelter. Or open your home to visiting missionaries and allow your kids to get to know people who are involved in meeting various needs around the world. We've usually been able to keep a guest room open at our house, and over the years many Christian workers have stayed with us. We never knew exactly what impact this would have on our children, but the cumulative impact seems to have been significant. Laurie is now married and serves in an international Christian ministry. Josh is studying biochemistry and volunteers each weekend in the emergency room of an inner-city hospital in Los Angeles.

A TEEN'S OWN ASSETS

While older kids should be brought into the process of giving from family assets, encourage them to also make their own significant gifts. A teenager who diligently saves and invests can acquire substantial assets (more on this in the following chapters), and some of these should be made available for giving. It's important that this not be a snap decision. While you could exercise a parental veto, it's probably better to just insist on a one- or two-week waiting period so your kids can be certain they want to follow through on a giving decision.

Last year my nephew Torrey achieved the dream of many teenage boys. He became the proud owner of a motor scooter. On hearing this news, even I felt a twinge of youthful envy, knowing how I had craved motor-powered devices of every kind at his age. Torrey enjoyed riding his scooter all over his Indiana neighborhood, until one day at church a visiting missionary read a list of needs from his mission agency. On the list was a motor scooter to transport an itinerant evangelist.

Torrey realized he had the means to answer that need. Since this would be a big gift, he brought his parents into the loop. He explained his desire to donate his motor scooter to the mission. His parents, wisely recognizing that this might prove a golden opportunity to exchange hardware for character, decided to support his decision.

This teenager had acquired the heart of a teenage philanthropist. He had seen beyond the me-centered vision of the marketers to an other-centered vision in which he could make a gift of lasting significance in the lives of others. Several weeks later he saw his motor scooter—now crated—loaded into a truck. Time passed, and Torrey heard how his gift had made a positive impact not only on the itinerant evangelist, but also in the lives of all the people who were affected by the evangelist's expanded ministry.

We want our kids to grow up to be openhanded, generous, caring individuals. But how can they escape all the societal pressure to spend, spend, spend? Helping give our kids a foundation by developing a generous character is only half of the equation. We also need to help them resist the siren call of "buy now!"

Surprisingly, one of our most potent allies is the humble piggy bank. In the next section we'll see how Justin can exchange a stack of worthless cereal-box promotions (plastic submarines powered by baking soda, for example) for something really worth having: the ability to save wisely.

PART IV

PRINCIPLE 3: SAVE WISELY

Chapter 13

The Power of Deferred Gratification

The Best Answer to "I Want It Now!"

Saving is not wildly popular in our high-speed, I-want-it-now culture. Most Americans, when they come unexpectedly into some money, have it spent in their minds even before they have the cash in their hands.

"Now we can take that dream vacation!" "Finally, we can dump this car and get that new Lexus we've had our eyes on!" Only a few adults have the ability to defer spending now in exchange for vastly increased options in the future. I won't ask which category you fall into—the key question is this: Which type of adult do you want your child to become?

Your children's future habits could actually have a direct effect on your own life. Imagine that you've finally retired, and your nest egg is more than enough to cover your living expenses, some travel, and all of your future medical needs. You look forward to your golden years filled with golf, good friends, those books you've always wanted to read, and perhaps some volunteer mission trips. It's finally time to enjoy a change of pace.

Now imagine that Justin, who unfortunately developed into an I-want-it-now kind of adult, comes to visit with his wife and kids. A short visit would be great, except they're not just visiting. Despite their surprisingly high incomes, Justin and his wife have spent their way through a fleet of vehicles, charged the maximum limit on enough credit cards to pave your patio, and refinanced the whole mess by means of a home-equity loan.

Unfortunately, they refinanced just after mortgage rates hit a temporary high and just before real estate values in their area slid off the cliff. They lost their house and declared bankruptcy, and now they've moved in with you "just until we can get back on our feet." You find yourself dreaming of a day that may never come, when your small house echoes with a blessed silence, absent the screams and whines of grandchildren whose charm has tarnished considerably with their prolonged proximity.

C'mon, that could *never* be you in thirty years. Your happy toddlers, cheerful softball-playing youngsters, or pimply, corsage-sporting prom goers could never become such financially inept adults, could they? You bet they could, and it's your mission to prevent it! You know exactly what you don't want: boomerang kids crashing into your peaceful retirement. But what is it that you *do* want for them? You want kids who will enter adulthood knowing how to save wisely, give generously, and spend carefully. In other words, openhanded people who manage God's wealth wisely.

In the previous section, we covered the character and habits of an openhanded giver. Now we'll tackle the second character trait our kids need to develop, the ability to defer a lesser good now in exchange for a greater good later. The ability to defer gratification is the foundation for success in all areas of wise financial management.

THE REALITY OF LIMITED POTENTIAL

Let's begin with a reality check: You have no control over your children's native aptitudes and abilities, and it's not true that all kids have limitless potential. Not every child has the gifts required to rise to the upper limits in earning potential. Some will do well just to be consistently employed.

Even the most gifted kids sometimes make choices in high school that can cut them off from many later-life options. Many kids decline to take geometry, calculus, advanced biology, or physics, little realizing that they're making decisions that will seriously restrict their future career options. They have unknowingly decided against the best jobs in engineering, medicine, and computer science just so this semester's coursework will be a little easier.

If so much decision-making power is in the hands of our kids, what's a parent to do? Plenty. You can build into their lives—by example and training—the ability to defer gratification. These two words reflect the biblical concept that forms the core of true wisdom—to be able to reasonably foresee the future options that will result from today's choices.

Deferred gratification is the key to producing money-savvy kids who grow into financially wise adults. If your children acquire no other financial training while under your care, this attribute alone will ensure that they will make better financial choices than most of their peers. And that's an awfully good success rate.

BALANCING THE SCALES

What does deferred gratification look like in real life? Here's a case study that demonstrates its power. Fifteen-year-old Sting (son of diehard fans of The Police, a now-defunct rock band from the 1980s with a lead singer named Sting) has been earning money through part-time jobs since he was thirteen. He has a four-figure nest egg invested in no-load mutual funds. In a few months he'll be sixteen, and with a driver's license he'll be able to travel around the city completely unsupervised. With his nest egg just sitting there earning money, he has given a lot of thought to the idea of buying a car. Who needs capital gains when you can have your own wheels?

The thought of owning your own car casts a powerful spell over teenagers. But Sting has made a surprising decision. He knows that a car would give him a lot more independence, and it would impress his friends—including the more popular girls at school. But he also knows that his savings would only buy a glorified beater, not a car that would rock the socks off a girl who's impressed by German engineering. Sting also understands that buying a car would consume all of his future teenage earnings just to pay for gas, maintenance, and insurance.

Looking beyond his immediate craving for a car, Sting sees how his nest egg could grow significantly by the time he heads off to college. He also recognizes that with a degree he could, upon graduation, buy something that would come much closer to his vision of a dream car. So Sting decides to borrow his parents' car when he needs transportation (much to their relief) and stakes his hopes of a supercool car on his postcollege career.

It takes a lot of character for a kid Sting's age to look into the distant future and decide to forego some high school thrills in exchange for a greater one in six long years. Sting had money in the bank, so why didn't he go ahead and get some wheels? He had plenty of pent-up yearning for a flashy, high-powered vehicle, so what caused him to wait? It's because he also had something else: a realistic expectation that he could have an even more gratifying chariot (babe-magnet-wise) if he opted for a college education first. Sting's parents started him on this path years earlier, long before he knew the difference between a Jeep and a Beemer.

DELIVERING GRATIFICATION

The ability to defer gratification is an incredibly versatile character quality, with applications outside the realm of giving, saving, and spending. When harnessed to your kids' natural potential, skills, and earning potential, it will help ensure that they live in a way that will contribute to their long-term good, not for short-lived pleasure. The quality of deferred gratification applies to a whole host of values and behaviors that you want your children to develop.

Think about the powerful hormones that kick in during adolescence. Eventually your doll-toting toddler will find herself wanting to be noticed by boys, and most of her peer group—not to mention product advertisers—will be urging her to "just do it." Why shouldn't she engage in premarital sex when every TV show, movie, magazine, and many of her friends seem to think it's a perfectly natural—and apparently highly enjoyable—activity? Your lone voice screaming a parental "No, *don't* do it!" will have little chance of rising above the shouting pro-sex crowd.

But wait, you've done a few things right. Starting when she was a toddler, you developed your daughter's ability to defer gratification. As she got older, you convinced her that sex is not only wonderful, it's beyond fantastic—but the ultimate enjoyment of that pleasure is experienced only in the context of marriage. Putting off a short-lived pleasure today enhances decades of tremendous pleasure later on after the wedding.

Why would a girl choose to believe this when she becomes a teenager and starts making her own decisions? It's because her parents understood something else about deferred gratification. For the deferral part to have any meaning, there must be eventual *gratification* of our desires. If tomorrow's enjoyment were likely to be less than today's, then we'd be fools to put off immediate pleasure. Kids need to know that there's a whole lifetime of wonderful sex down the road—if they don't mess it up for themselves before they're married.

That's why we need to help our kids learn the reward of deferring momentary pleasures in other ways while they are children. The same principle applies to anything in life that's worth doing. As we help our children exchange limited short-term pleasures for superior long-term rewards, there must be regular seasons of gratification, or else the whole lesson is lost. Think of a poor donkey pulling a cart, enticed onward by the carrot hanging a short distance in front of his nose. If that donkey never got to actually eat the carrot, he might as well sit down and defy his master's wrath.

Our kids are a lot smarter than donkeys (though sometimes they approach a mule's stubbornness), and we need to show them that a pleasure deferred is not a pleasure forsaken—only put away temporarily so it can be enhanced. If we can build this characteristic into our kids, the long-term developments can be wonderful.

Let's get back to Sting, the teenager who decided to keep his money in a mutual fund. He graduated from high school and entered college, where he acquired a taste for computer science. He graduated with a degree in business and got an entry-level position in a Fortune 500 technology company. Then he blew a year's salary on an absurdly showy BMW. But apart from that one unnecessary extravagance, he has lived carefully beneath his income while investing the difference. And he gives a surprising amount each year to his church and favorite charitable organizations.

Sting married a lovely girl, and now they have teenage children of their own, are debt-free, own their home, and between their investments and company retirement plans, Sting could retire early if he wasn't having such a good time as chief technology officer for his company. If Sting were your son, whenever he came to your house for a visit you wouldn't turn off the lights and pretend you weren't home. You'd throw a party. You'd enjoy cookouts, rounds of golf, an occasional movie. You'd go to church together and enjoy all the fun and fellowship that one can have with adult children of whom you're proud.

Having your children grow up to become money-savvy adults is a beautiful dream. It can become reality if you get busy now and start helping it to become a reality. In the next few chapters we'll see how the art of deferring gratification is best learned through good financial management. And what's a kid's first experience with saving? Usually it's the piggy bank—you know, the kind that gets smashed when you want to spend its contents. In the next chapter we'll see why we'd be better off smashing it now—*before* putting anything inside.

Chapter 14

The Trouble with the Piggy Bank

Break It Now! Go Ahead

One of our more short-lived pets was a hamster that sojourned with us for only a few weeks before departing suddenly and inexplicably for that great Exercise Wheel in the Sky. While he was part of our family, we marveled at his two chief talents: the ability to navigate our house while scampering inside a transparent plastic sphere, and the art of stuffing a week's worth of hamster food into his cheeks all at once.

Hamsters are natural-born savers, as are most animals that have to gather their food during the warmer months and then live through a barren winter in some underground burrow. A few kids seem to enter the world with a hamster gene, saving everything they can, but most need to be trained in the basics of saving.

We saw in the last chapter that learning to defer gratification is one of the greatest abilities we can encourage in our offspring. The skill of deferred gratification is often perfected through saving. Likewise, the ability to defer gratification makes saving possible. The key to helping kids understand the significance of saving is to help them realize that the *future enjoyment of their money is indeed better than present consumption.* This is why I advise all parents to smash the piggy bank even before their kids put any money into it. The time-honored piggy bank fails completely in the area of making clear the future benefit of saving. With a piggy bank, the assets go in, but they never come out. Where's the fun in that?

Even the dimmest child understands that the quarters and dollars he puts into piggy banks could be exchanged today for video games, Pokémon cards, comic books, or whatever he craves at his age. The mere fact that the traditional piggy bank doesn't even have a mechanism for the extraction of the money shows the pointlessness of this type of saving. "I could get something really good with this money," grumbles Justin as he reluctantly feeds the piggy bank, "but instead I have to save it." There are much more effective ways to make saving attractive to our young children.

PROVING THAT SAVING PAYS

The trick of hooking young kids on saving is to set up an artificial system so they can experience compelling rewards from saving—big enough rewards to offset the lost pleasure of immediate consumption. Imagine that your four-year-old is hooked on pudding. His day brightens noticeably at the prospect of pulling the top off a pudding container, and he smiles broadly the entire time he's spooning it down.

Let's say he gets back home from a hard three hours at preschool. He spent the morning naming shapes, learning to not run with scissors, and snacking on white paste. You set before him a can of pudding and explain, "Now Justin, you can either have this pudding now or after your nap. If you wait until after your nap, you can have it with one of your favorite cookies while you watch a *Veggie Tales* video. Which would you prefer?"

Many kids would begin to whine for both the pudding *and* the cookie to be served right now! But if you firmly ward off that possibility, you may gain some insights into Justin's nature. By creating an artificial situation that makes clear the benefits of deferred gratification, you have a chance to teach little Justin an important lesson. Can he resist the present lure of pudding in order to get the magic combination of pudding *with a cookie* later? If not, let's imagine that Justin has gobbled his pudding and had his nap. Now it's time for a video—without a snack.

Since he opted for eating his pudding earlier rather than having it now with a cookie, you take advantage of an opportunity to demonstrate the value of deferring gratification. You bring out a plate with his favorite cookie plus a container of pudding. But instead of serving the snack to the eager little guy, you instead announce: "Justin, do you remember when you got home from preschool and I said you could have a cookie with your pudding if you waited until after your nap? This is what you would have gotten. I'm afraid I'll have to put it away, but you might want to have it after your nap tomorrow." Then, even while little Justin screams and throws a fit, you calmly put it all away.

To teach young children about deferred gratification, there must first be a genuine choice. Most kids would like pudding now *and* later with a cookie. Really assertive ones would demand a cookie and pudding now, lobby to skip the nap, and then insist on having both snacks again with a video! It's your job to structure your children's life so they have a real choice, and one that can't be altered by whining, sulking, or throwing a tantrum.

The second condition for building the ability to defer gratification is to ensure that the deferred delight must be as real as the present pleasure. The young child who opts for pudding now has the experience of enjoying real pudding in the present. The future is still an abstract concept to him. But by bringing out the pudding-later option with a cookie, so the child can see it, you make the future pleasure as real and as tangible as the pudding that Justin gulped earlier that day.

But isn't it cruel to bring out the bigger treat that Justin could have had later and then not allow him to enjoy it right now? Perhaps it sounds cruel, but if a young child is going to learn the true value of deferred gratification, his parents have to make clear what the bigger enjoyment would have been if the child had waited.

THE SAVING JAR

As a child gets older, he's ready to start an actual saving program. It helps to set up a saving target using a scheme similar to the giving jars discussed in chapter 11. In addition to decorating jars for collecting donations to various charities, you also decorate a special jar for savings.

Imagine that Justin is now eight, and he wants a new game cartridge for his PlayStation. Instead of saying, "Ask your grandmother to get it for your birthday," you create a savings plan targeting the game cartridge. You wash out a jelly jar, decorate it with advertising cutouts depicting the desired game cartridge, and put it in Justin's room near his giving jars.

Have a short planning time so he can see that it is indeed feasible to save for his goal. I'll assume that Justin gets an allowance of seven dollars per week (an amount I chose so I could simplify the math in this example). Let's also assume that the bulk of his allowance is discretionary money and not required for school supplies and other necessities. If he distributes one dollar among his giving jars, he can decide for himself if he wants to save the remaining six dollars each week and reach his goal in a month, or save less and buy the game cartridge after a longer time.

You can increase the impact of the lesson by introducing incentives. To make aggressive saving the most attractive proposition, tell Justin that if he saves at least half of his allowance toward an agreed-upon goal, you'll add an extra two dollars to his savings jar every week. Or if he saves enough money so that his goal is three-quarters met within four weeks, you'll spring for the difference.

These incentives produce two positive effects. First, Justin acquires the motivation to do the math required to evaluate the alternatives. Second, he's rewarded in proportion to the intensity with which he saves. In both cases, the abstract future becomes clearer, progressively closer, and finally arrives in the form of what he so greatly desires.

Now when you give Justin his allowance, he gladly stuffs a portion of it into his saving jar. He knows that setting aside just a few dollars a week will result in significant sums. In a month or so he'll have enough to buy a game cartridge.

Justin may not yet have a grasp on the math he'll need to really understand the power of saving. The jar provides a picture of his money growing, but it's not a precise measurement. How does money grow over time, and how can a kid learn the significance of seasons of financial growth? In the next chapter we'll look at simple ways to help kids acquire what people used to call a "head for figures."

Chapter 15

Getting Chummy
with Numbers

Don't Let a Fear of Math Get in the Way

A few years ago a major toy manufacturer blundered into the thickets of sexism by marketing a long-haired blond doll that whined, "Math is *hard!*" Even overlooking the fact that most parents have heard that complaint from children of both sexes, the company certainly deserved the drubbing it received. But the critics of the math-challenged doll bypassed the obvious issue: Math might be hard, but it's essential for financial maturity.

My children spanned the spectrum from the mathematically gifted to the more typical kid who's thankful that after completing calculus in college, he or she will never have to utter the words "integral" and "function" in the same sentence again. Most parents are in the second category, and many of us didn't even take calculus.

Math phobia will make it tough for many of us to teach our

children the basic math they need to become financially competent adults. Like it or not, there are foundational mathematical skills that pave the way for successful saving, giving, and spending. The good news is that we don't need to know how to extract square roots, solve differential equations, or even answer the "train leaving Chicago at sixty miles per hour" problem. What we do need are some basic concepts, such as how to work with percentages and fractions, and the motivation to pass these concepts on to our children.

As you pass on the concepts, do it with vision, as in "the ability to see." Help your kids view numbers in a way that makes concrete sense to them. Most very young children have a grasp of numbers that corresponds exactly to the number of fingers (and sometimes toes) that they possess. Children who are three years old can hold up three fingers to indicate their age. What do they hold up when they are three and a half? Yep, still three—they can't visualize the concept of a half year in their fingers.

Yet I'm convinced that children can learn fractions at a very early age. "Hey—his piece is bigger than mine!" is ironclad proof that little Justin can tell the difference between a piece of cake evenly divided into halves or one calculated to favor his sister. The cake made a fraction visible, which is the key to teaching basic arithmetic to young children.

SIMPLE MATH GAMES

Let's start with a simple illustration of the power of multiplication. A wealthy rajah was so enamored with the game of chess that he promised the inventor any reward he named. The clever inventor said, "I only want a single grain of rice, your majesty, placed on the first square of my chessboard. Then I'd like two on the second square, four on the next square, eight on the next, and so on until the entire sixty-four squares are covered."

According to legend, the arithmetically challenged rajah gladly authorized the reward without realizing the power of geometric multiplication. His advisors would have told him there's not enough rice in the world to complete the task, and the value of such a quantity of rice far exceeded the value of the rajah's entire kingdom.

You can create a similar visual illustration with an empty egg carton and a few cups of uncooked rice. Explain the story of the rajah and the chessboard, and challenge little Justin to try the same thing using only twelve spaces to hold rice (assuming the egg carton was designed for a dozen eggs). Most children will breeze through the 1, 2, 4, 8, 16, and 32 stages and get overwhelmed at the 64, 128, or 256 level. And there are still three egg spaces left to fill!

There are many ways that important mathematical concepts can be worked into playtime. Think of this as a financial Head Start program for kids. In Head Start, the goal is not reading but "reading readiness." The kids play in ways that give them familiarity with shapes, colors, and the concepts of quantity and order. You want to do exactly the same thing with numbers.

For simple math games, it's hard to beat good old Play-Doh (or its homemade equivalent). Encourage Tyra to create a Play-Doh pizza parlor where you and other family members can order pizzas. Then order three pizzas split up six ways, or two pizzas divided equally for four friends. Or add a twist. Order one big pizza for you and Tyra, except your share needs to be twice as big as hers.

Another kitchen-based form of math play involves stringing macaroni. Let the smaller macaroni pieces be the equivalent of the number one, while the bigger elbows are ten. Use these to put together strings that represent various numbers such as your house address, telephone numbers, the names of pets (where the letter *A* equals one, *B* equals two, etc.). Such tally strings were actually used in ancient cultures to keep track of financial records.

If you occasionally get your kids a candy treat, consider buying a package of Skittles or M&Ms. Say, "I'll get you a pack of Skittles, but you have to do something before you can eat the candy. I want to know how many Skittles are in a bag." After your child counts the candy, write down the number. Then the next time you offer to buy Skittles, make the offer more complicated. "I'll get you a bag of Skittles, but I want to know how many of each color there are." If the kids are old enough, have them calculate the percentages for each color. Now make the game more complicated. The next time you offer to buy a package of Skittles, say, "Let's all predict how many red Skittles will be in this bag. The one who gets closest gets to eat an extra 10 percent."

The grocery store is a fantastic place to help your kids become mathematically aware. Have them weigh produce, check the price per unit of weight, and then figure out how much each item costs. Show them how to use the store labeling to understand concepts such as price-per-ounce and volume discount. Allow them to figure out the savings with percent-off coupons.

Simple table games are also wonderful for developing basic financial or arithmetic instincts. Yahtzee is excellent for building numerical awareness, and it's tough to beat Monopoly when it comes to mimicking the financial realities of life. Most kids first become aware of concepts such as taxes, payday, rent, home owner-ship, and mortgages through playing this venerable game.

And don't neglect the resources available in educationally ori-ented toy stores and school-supply stores. During our years in Asia we kept Josh supplied with math workbooks that he enjoyed so much that he would pitch a fit if we tried to take them away.

Math in School

I made a fatal discovery partway through the third grade. The pub-lisher of my arithmetic textbook, rather than printing a separate teacher's edition with homework answers in the back, had created a system whereby the answer to one question was hidden in the format of the following question. Once I had figured this out, I completed all my homework with perfect accuracy and in record time. My teacher considered me a math genius, at least for the third grade.

The fourth grade was a different story. To my shock, our new textbook stubbornly refused to reveal the answer to my homework any other way than by working the problems. And for most of the third grade I had paid absolutely no attention to how to work the problems. I began to fail math, my teacher regarded me as a near-idiot, and I added stuttering to my list of dubious accomplish-ments. It was not a good year.

When your kids begin school, monitor their math homework. Make sure they get the kind of help they need to keep up. It may simply involve encouragement, math games, workbooks, or tutor-ing. Don't fall for the "When will I ever *need* this?" line that causes so many to quit math. Having a strong foundation in math means expanded career options, and the opposite precludes a host of wonderful occupations.

I know exactly what the vilified doll meant when she whimpered, "Math is hard." It's hard for most of us. Even Alexander the Great, despite while a youth having the inestimable advantage of learning math from none other than Aristotle, complained about its difficulty. He felt that there should be an easy version for royal offspring, such as himself! Alexander was rebuked with the words, "There is no royal road to geometry!" We all have to learn it the hard way, but we can at least pave the path for our children with fun learning experiences.

The payoff is worth it. With a basic competence in math, everything in your children's life takes on more richness. They'll have the skills to understand the difference between a good deal and a bad deal, a wise investment and a foolish one. And believe me, they're going to make plenty of foolish ones! Many parents aren't comfortable themselves with full-fledged investment vehicles, let alone teaching their kids about investments.

In the next chapter we'll look at some easy steps to make investments interesting to kids, and maybe you'll learn something as well. So pour yourself a cold glass of diet cola, open a bag of chips, and we'll look at some ways to bring grown-up investments down to kid level.

Chapter 16

Investment Basics
for Third Graders

Help for Parents Who Get Nervous Around Mutual Funds

Kids like to poke around and look for treasure, and at the age of
five I was no different. I went out in our yard with some grade-
school friends and, under our porch, struck gold. Actually it was
silver—a big jar full of half dollars and silver dollars. I was thrilled
with my discovery but remarkably uninformed about its value. I
didn't even recognize that the larger coins were real money, thinking they were something like the St. Christopher medals worn by
my Catholic friends.

Before my parents discovered my loot, apparently buried and
forgotten by a former owner of our home, I had given away as much
as 20 percent of the "worthless" bigger coins. When my parents
confiscated what remained, it soon was spent on a new bedroom

set for my brother and me that we used until we finally went off to college.

It's hard to imagine a modern little Justin being as naive about money as I was, but when it comes to investing, most children need a basic grounding in the fundamentals. What kills kids' enthusiasm for saving beyond attaining short-term goals (a new game for the PlayStation) is the problem of helping them visualize the potential growth in even modest long-term investments. Putting money into a long-term investment means you don't have access to the money for a long time. In a child's scale of time, that's an eternity.

But once your child builds up a certain amount of savings, it's time to start directing her toward some investments that she can grasp. The best method I've found is to maintain a variety of savings tools—banks, if you will, dedicated toward specific saving goals. This is similar to the savings-jar concept discussed in chapter 14. It enables kids to designate a portion of their savings toward a short-term goal while deferring the remainder to a much later date. The deferred amount is invested.

In the traditional scenario, the contents of the piggy bank get deposited into a low-interest passbook account. I wouldn't wish this on any child. Any right-thinking kid would scream bloody murder to see his hard-saved coins disappearing—forever, from his point of view—into such an account. A kid who has been faithfully saving needs to see his jars full of quarters exchanged for real, growth-oriented investments. This is when you start teaching your kids some investment basics.

Thanks to advances in investment possibilities, your kids have a choice of interesting places to invest their savings. I've already stressed the need for kids to be able to visualize their savings goals, and that they be as tangible as possible. Well, there's nothing as tangible as real estate! You can walk on it, sift its dirt through your fingers, build forts on it—it's totally real. But it's not practical for kids to exchange their rolls of nickels and quarters for real estate. A superior alternative is to invest in companies with a high degree of visibility from a child's point of view.

Most financial advisors advocate companies that produce products kids use: Nike, McDonald's, and Sony, for example. So discuss with your child all the products that he uses in daily life. Make a list of the brands and companies that those products represent. Include toy stores, bookstores, clothing manufacturers, retail outlets, and chains. Now talk through the list and find out which ones he regards most highly. You might be surprised to find out that he has definite opinions that could actually influence your choice of one company over another. Finally, focus in on a single company for Justin's first share of stock.

Now it's time to explain the meaning of owning stock. While children can imagine buying a Happy Meal at McDonald's, or even a dozen such enjoyable repasts, they might have a hard time imagining what it means to own a share of McDonald's. Just ask little Justin who owns McDonald's. If he doesn't say Ronald, then explain that lots of people own it all together, sort of the way that he and his sister share ownership in their swing set. In other words, it's owned by the shareholders, and Justin can be one too! Or he can be a part owner of Reebok or Sony or Disney.

Some parents might argue that it would be more logical for a child to buy shares in a mutual fund rather than speculative shares in a single company. It's true that putting all your eggs in one basket may not be the wisest investment strategy, but the goal here is to make investing real from a kid's point of view. It's tough enough for a child to envision the significance of a share of Sony, let alone a mutual fund containing thousands of individual stocks.

But isn't it wrong to encourage our children to gamble with their money by buying speculative stocks? Some would argue that the only safe place for a child's money is in savings bonds or certificates of deposit. But such an argument misses the point. We want to teach important ideas about investing, and the benefits of owning shares of individual companies make it worth the risk.

If your child catches the vision and buys into the idea of exchanging his jars of coins for shares of stock, how do you actually do it? I can imagine the result of slamming a bagful of quarters on the counter at the local office of Merrill Lynch, Pierce, Fenner & Smith and announcing, "Kirsten here wants all the shares of Sony this money will buy!" (That would be an interesting experiment, by the way.)

One problem with full-service brokerage accounts is that they typically require a sizable amount of money simply to open an account—two thousand dollars and up would be typical. Another problem is that most traders want to work with round numbers. Buying a hundred shares of Sony for Justin would be no problem, but buying a single share would cause, at the least, raised eyebrows. A third deterrent to this method of buying small amounts of stock is the broker's commission. Even a deep-discount brokerage firm would charge (assuming you had an account) at least five dollars per trade—a hefty premium to pay when your share might have a value well below one hundred dollars.

A better solution is to buy stock through a little-known

method that enables investors to buy small quantities—even individual shares—directly from the company. Known as DRIP (Direct Re-Investment Program) accounts, these are maintained by many corporations for the convenience of small investors who don't want to pay commissions to brokers. DRIP investments are perfect for moving your kid's piggy bank coins into the next level of investing, since the cash outlay can be as small as ten dollars. Your child can buy a single share, pay no commission, and have the privilege of being a shareholder in a great company.

The DRIP approach does have one disadvantage when it comes to making corporate entities tangible to our children. Investors usually don't receive stock certificates with DRIP accounts—not, that is, unless you pay substantial fees for the privilege. But don't worry—you can always make your own certificates, and they can be *way* cooler than the ones turned out by the corporate graphics department.

Now is when you combine your kid's investment with an enjoyable craft project! Turn Justin's first share of stock into a wonderful wall decoration that includes the company's name, logo (cut-and-paste comes in handy here), and perhaps cutouts of their major products all pasted in a colorful, childlike, but—best of all—highly visual whole. And be sure to include Justin's name prominently as owner. You might want to consider making the area that displays the number of shares in a way that allows additional shares to be represented later.

The result is not only a wonderful bedroom decoration, it's a full-time reminder that your child's investments are at work with ShoeBok, Waldo World, or Pineapple Republic. If you succeed in making intangible investing become concrete, Justin will look at stores, products, and services in a whole new way—a way that will, in time, reflect adult investment attitudes.

Bear in mind that many publicly held corporations are engaged in practices you might find objectionable, either on moral or ethical grounds or due to environmental concerns. Be sure that you and your children check out the companies before you buy shares of stock. You don't want to find out later that your supposedly kid-friendly corporation is actually the world's largest producer of tobacco, fortified wine, or pornography.

A kid's jar full of change, if allowed to grow, can become real money someday. Remember that bedroom set my parents bought with the buried treasure I found under the porch? If they had put that cash into an investment account that averaged 11 percent from the year I found it to the time I write these words, it would now be worth—hold on to your hat—more than fifty-five thousand dollars.[1]

There's a downside to this kind of investment success, of course, and it's known by the three little words "Internal Revenue Service." Yes, your children may have to pay taxes on their investment income as well as their earned income. And it's not simple, either! Congress, in its infinite wisdom, has seen fit to make the rules on taxation of minors among the most complex in the tax law. The bottom line (at least as I write this), however, is that your dependent child needs to file a tax return if he or she has unearned income of more than seven hundred dollars or total gross income in excess of forty-three hundred dollars. But don't let the penalty of success discourage you from helping your children become involved in investing. After all, earning money and paying taxes on it certainly beats *not* earning money.

Third graders who save their quarters can become teenagers with significant financial assets. In the next chapter we'll take a look at what a teenage Justin can do to continue developing his understanding of grown-up investment opportunities—and without falling into the trap of peer-influenced materialism.

Chapter 17

I Am Justin's Investment Portfolio

Help Your Child Grow with the Market

My best friend had a wonderful golden retriever named Griffin. This dog liked nothing better than to go for a sedate walk in the park. Because there was a leash law, Griffin was always wearing a leash—*wearing* being the operative word. He trotted obediently alongside his master while holding his rolled-up leash in his mouth!

Griffin also possessed a near superhuman (for a dog, that is) power of deferring gratification. You could balance a dog biscuit on his muzzle for hours, and he wouldn't think of snapping it off his nose and down the hatch until given the go-ahead by some authority figure. Griffin resisted the urge to immediately munch the dog biscuit in favor of a greater deferred satisfaction—the praise and companionship of his master.

This same level of self-control is something we want to build into our teenagers. We want them to be able to put off an immediate pleasure for a greater deferred satisfaction. There's one big difference, though, between Griffin and our human teenagers (I mean other than the fact that our teens eat a lot more). Griffin always depended on an external signal to determine when he could gobble his treats. He lacked an internal monitor that said, "I won't gulp this down just yet" or "Now's the time. I'm gonna go for it!"

That internal gauge is an essential factor in building money-savvy yet character-rich teenagers. If our kids have been diligently saving and investing during their preteen years, and if they keep it up until they're fourteen or fifteen, they may have accumulated a sizable amount of assets. How do we keep them growing in their ability to defer gratification? After all, a kid who's broke has fairly few options, no matter how much he craves the latest PlayStation. It's a different story, though, for a kid who knows that his savings and investments could buy a dozen PlayStations without tapping out his assets.

INVESTING FOR THE LONG HAUL

In the last chapter we figured out how to help a child purchase his first share of stock. The goal now is to keep him interested as a teenager, when a colorful, homemade stock certificate poster is no longer enough to motivate him to keep his money invested for the long haul. The key, of course, is to keep on painting the picture of what Justin's investments really represent. It's not just a certificate on the wall or the numbers listed in his investment account. His investments represent future possibilities and options that wouldn't exist if he were to use those assets to buy a motorcycle.

Although he doesn't give much thought to his future as an adult, if you pressed him, Justin would acknowledge that some day he'd like to get married and own a home. We can help him understand that his investments, if allowed to grow, could provide the down payment for a house when he's older. It's almost inconceivable that a teen would think about the cost of educating his future children or planning for his retirement in fifty years. That's why we're there—to keep talking about a future that is unimaginably remote to a fifteen-year-old.

One way to keep teens motivated about investing is to bring them into discussions about family investments. This could be as simple as a dinnertime conversation. "Kids, we've got some money to invest this month. What companies do you like?" Talk about the pros and cons of each company that is mentioned. Compare competitors, marketing advantages, current market valuations, and earning prospects. This doesn't have to be boringly technical, but it's a great time for making sure that your kids understand the basic concepts involved in being shareholders in major corporations. If you need a refresher course yourself, consider the excellent online educational resources at the Web sites of the major brokerage houses *(http://www.ml.com; http://www.schwab.com)*, as well as introductory books such as Eric Tyson's *Investing for Dummies* (1999).

As you have this discussion, make sure you bring in other factors that teens will want to consider. Is the company a major polluter of the environment? Does the company provide a needed product or service, or does it make its profits off useless or even morally harmful materials? Is the company known for unfair labor practices, either in this country or overseas? Teenagers are still calibrating their moral compass, and they need to think about the bigger picture when it comes to investing in large corporations.

Money talk, whether it's about the stock market or corporate ethics, is often boring to kids when it stays in the realm of the abstract. It becomes much more relevant when it touches on their world. So tie your discussions into their life experience. Which is the better investment, Gap or Abercrombie & Fitch? Is this a good time to buy either one, or if not, which other high-quality companies are more likely to see an increase in business? What trends do we notice that could represent an investment opportunity (for example, the growing market for broadband media access), or should we consider moving our money out of existing investments—for either financial or ethical reasons?

Another way to keep your kids interested is to create a family competition. Divide into teams and issue each team ten thousand dollars in play money. Have each team put together its theoretical investment portfolio. The team with the best results after three months wins the right to determine how some of the family's real money will be invested.

PERSONAL RESPONSIBILITY

When you bring your teens into discussions about investing and family finances, they inevitably learn something about your actual assets. You don't, however, want them to get the notion that your family is rich, because it will greatly reduce any motivation they may feel to save and invest for their own future. Sometimes teenagers have a very shaky understanding of what constitutes wealth, and may mistakenly think their family is loaded when there's not even enough in investments to fund a full year of college! It's not appropriate for children to know all about their parents' financial affairs—or even be able to estimate their net worth. So keep the details of your finances under lock and key, or password protected, and please—use a kid-proof password (and don't write it on the bottom of your mouse pad)!

And need I mention that you insist that your kids not speak of their finances outside the family circle? You really don't want Justin's friends to know his net worth, let alone anything about your family's investments. Teach your children to deflect prying questions about financial assets tactfully yet firmly.

Teenagers should feel a growing responsibility to prepare for their own financial future. You don't want them to assume they can rely on your assets to stake their financial success as adults, but make sure you let them know that you'll do all you can to help them acquire a college education. Beyond that, they're on their own. "Don't plan on an inheritance," you might say in passing. "What we don't spend we'll probably give away." You can always change your mind later, depending on how your kids wind up managing their own money.

These practices will help your kids recognize that their daily choices as teenagers are significant. Sure, their parents are helping to launch them into life, but succeeding in adult life will be up to them. This approach pays dividends in helping your teens see finances as something other than a way to purchase Palm Pilots and Prada purses. It helps them begin to see that current investments truly are a head start on their future earnings.

A Parent's Example

Much of what will stick in your teens' minds is what they observe you doing. Kids are likely to catch the attitudes of their parents, and a proper attitude toward money is no exception. If you're making impulsive decisions, frequently upgrading your lifestyle, and spending every dime you earn, you're teaching your kids to do the same—regardless of how much you verbally endorse a financially responsible lifestyle.

If, on the other hand, they see us choosing to live at a specific level regardless of our assets, and they see us making decisions on charitable giving as carefully as we make our investment decisions, they will likely adopt attitudes that are consistent with biblical values. We want our teenagers to understand three crucial truths about finances. First, all of "our" assets really belong to God. Second, we're managers, not owners, of those assets. And finally, we receive wealth from God in order to give, save, and spend wisely. All of this is possible only because of God's generosity toward us.

Even if your kids reach adulthood dead broke, if you've helped them form a character derived from these attitudes, you can pat yourself on the back—vigorously. The goal of teaching your children investment basics isn't so much to help them make a pile of money, but to make the most of their character—especially to defer an immediate gratification for a larger, more wonderful satisfaction at a later time.

The best scenario of all is for our kids to wind up like my friend's dog, Griffin. He loved his walks as well as his doggie treats, yet the praise and companionship of his master were the things for which he really lived. If we can use investment training to help our children's character grow and mature and to help them draw closer to their Master, we'll help them win twice. Ultimately they'll hear their Master (and ours) welcome them into a heavenly home—not with doggie treats, but with the praise and fellowship of a life well lived in the center of God's love.

Learning to put off today's pleasure in order to save and invest is one of the toughest lessons a child can learn. But what about spending? Come on—*nobody* needs lessons in spending, do they? In the next chapter we'll see that learning to spend carefully isn't as simple as it seems.

PART V

PRINCIPLE 4: SPEND CAREFULLY

Chapter 18

A Positive View of Consequences

Choices Lead to Results—Both Good and Bad

One children's story that has been unofficially banned from the modern public school classroom is the classic "The Little Red Hen." The gist of the tale is that the red hen repeatedly invited a number of other animals to join her in preparing something good to eat. She received no takers, except when it was time to eat the yummy thing she had made single-handedly, or perhaps single-wingedly. Then she was faced with a predicament. Should she invite the animals that earlier refused to help to come now and sit at her table for a well-rounded meal?

The Little Red Hen could have said, "It's really okay that you didn't lift a finger to help make this treat, and in order to prove that your unwillingness to work can't be held against you, come on and dig in anyway!" But that's not how the children's classic reads. The

Little Red Hen in fact offered a pithy comment that wasn't too different from what the apostle Paul wrote in 2 Thessalonians 3:10: "If a man will not work, he shall not eat." In other words, our choices have definite consequences.[1]

So far, I have emphasized the positive strategies for helping children develop the ability to defer gratification. For instance, giving your preschooler pudding *and* a cookie after her nap is a positive reward for her decision to delay the treat until after she took her nap. In terms of carrot-and-stick motivations, enjoying the pleasure of eating the carrot is a much more effective motivation than being punished with the stick. A child develops internal discipline as she associates voluntary deprivation with an anticipated and superior outcome a little later.

But while we emphasize the motivational carrot, what about the metaphorical stick? It has its uses, especially when a child is old enough to suffer the natural consequences of his unwise choices. In adult life, a failure to make wise financial choices has definite repercussions. It's far better for kids to obtain this knowledge now. Better to learn from a small mistake as a child than to wait and learn the lesson later in life when the consequences can be devastating.

Remember the option little Justin, as a preschooler, was given in chapter 14? He could choose to have some pudding now, or he could wait until after his nap and enjoy a cookie with his pudding. The immediate delight would come sooner, but without the added pleasure of a cookie. If Justin chose the pudding-now option, a wise parent would help him realize what he missed. The parent could make the deferred option tangible later by showing Justin a bowl of pudding with a cookie on the side. Of course, he's likely to throw a world-class tantrum, but the ultimate outcome would be an increased ability to evaluate the relative wisdom of choosing an immediate satisfaction or postponing it for a demonstrably better one later. In other words, when his parents showed him the cookie and pudding combination that he had declined, Justin was getting a dose of "the stick."

I'm not suggesting being needlessly cruel to our kids. It's just that at the earlier ages they don't have the perceptual development to evaluate the wisdom of relative choices. The carrot is a somewhat contrived and parentally assisted method of helping children make wise choices, and the stick is making sure they live with the consequences when they make poor choices.

As children gain access to money, they will always be faced with the immediate option of spending it. By allowing your kids to make certain spending decisions on their own, you're giving them the opportunity to experience the consequences of their spending—both good and bad. I'm not advising that children be allowed free rein to spend their assets in any way they choose. There will always be prohibitions (no drugs, alcohol, or dynamite, for example) and limitations on how much they can spend. They shouldn't be allowed to raid their college fund to buy a junk car, a common scenario that I'll discuss later as a prime financial disaster to avoid.

On the other hand, those assets that are not designated for giving and saving are theirs to control. You give them that freedom so they can learn to make wise spending decisions now that will carry over into their adult life. The question at hand is this: What constitutes a wise decision?

KIDS WILL BE KIDS

Sometimes we consider a given expenditure unwise purely because we've lost the childlike joy of seeing toys through a child's eyes. We mustn't discourage our kids from being kids! I remember vividly the vast array of cheap candies—gumballs, licorice whips, jelly worms, wax bottles filled with neon-colored goo—that I once craved. The difference is that now the thought of slurping up even one red licorice vine comes near to turning my stomach. But that's an adult perspective.

When Laurie and Josh were at the age when no candy was too vile to be the object of yearning, I was forced to come to grips with their child's perspective. Their favorite was a ring pop, a giant candy jewel affixed to a one-size-fits-all plastic finger ring. They liked the convenience and security of the ring, and the large size and near indissolubility of the hard candy meant it would last for hours—or even weeks if it was accidentally misplaced and then found later.

We need to let our kids be kids. When the one thing they want is a new game for their PlayStation, we need to graciously let them make their choices. When you think of it, you can't lose. If they make a good choice, well, that's good! And if they make a poor choice—aha, another important lesson to be learned.

It's hard for parents to allow their children to learn from negative consequences. We have an instinct to protect our offspring from the consequences of poor choices. But our goal is to raise children with a sterling character. When kids learn that they *have* to live with their bad choices, they develop the inward strength to make better choices that will serve them well in the independent years of adulthood.

Let's say Justin has been saving for several weeks to buy a particular video game. When his parents finally take him to the store, he finds that he's five dollars short. However, there's another game that he's not familiar with that is priced within his means. What does he do? What do his parents do?

Here's what you, as a parent, should *not* do. You should never lend Justin the money to buy the game he really wants. You don't want him to learn the seductive joys of buy-now pay-later. It won't hurt him to save his money for a few more weeks. And giving him an advance on his allowance has disastrous consequences, not the least of which is that it insulates Justin from the consequences of his choices. It sets a precedent in which he'll expect you to come to the rescue every time his poor planning leads to a disappointment.

One option available to Justin is to simply walk away with his money in his pocket. If he chooses this option, rejoice! Your son is beginning to learn to defer gratification. His goal to save up for a game cartridge requires this type of dedication and commitment. You should verbally express your appreciation. "That's a very wise decision. You'll have what you need in no time. How would you like some frozen yogurt?" When he finally saves up the additional five dollars, consider making a special trip to get the game, and make sure that his persistence is appropriately celebrated.

Another choice available to Justin is to make a substitute purchase with the money he has. While the decision is being made— and Justin is open to input—you could help him process the issues by asking a few questions: "Are you sure you'll like playing this other game? How much more money do you need to get the game you really want? How long would it take to save up the difference?" But it's important that the decision be his to make.

If Justin decides to buy the cheaper game, he might get home and find that he has wasted his money on a game that is deservedly despised by all right-thinking kids his age. Instead of the lifelike three-dimensional graphics that made his original choice such a state-of-the-art game, he wound up with some repackaged antique with glitzy and misleading cover art. Justin knows he blew it.

No matter how disappointed Justin becomes, control your parental instincts to "make it all better." At the same time, resist any urge to say, "I told you to wait! But would you listen to me? No-o-o. You just *had* to buy this worthless, second-rate piece of junk. Yada-yada-yada."

Don't waste the important lesson that Justin is learning. His unwise decision may reinforce his ability to say no to a future buying opportunity. He's simply experiencing the "stick" aspect of learning to postpone an immediate ho-hum purchase for a much more enjoyable purchase at a more appropriate time—such as when he's saved up the rest of the money he needs.

Believe it or not, a series of painful lessons like this one will help him become the kind of adult who saves up to pay cash for a car, then finds one at a reasonable price. It will keep him from being the kind of person who drops into an auto dealership "just to look" at the latest overpriced hot sports car and two hours later drives away in a car that has most of his future earnings tied up in a high-interest auto loan.

Lessons like these—the ones that build character for a lifetime—can be bought much more cheaply when the kids are young. Negative experiences, when they are carefully controlled, can help children learn the ABCs of money management. But to make spending decisions of any sort, kids have to have money to spend. That's one reason an allowance is useful. Properly managed, an allowance can provide a child with regular opportunities to learn wisdom in how she spends a portion of her money.

In the next chapter we'll take a comprehensive look at how to deal with allowances: when to begin them, how much is appropriate, and what we want to achieve by giving our kids an allowance.

Chapter 19

What's Great About Allowances

Four Principles That Make Allowances Work

Kevin's parents were among the first to make a fortune in tech stocks in the early 1980s. That explains why he's always had whatever he wished for. Now twenty-four, Kevin has owned more than a dozen automobiles (he wrecked three of them). He has hosted all-night parties for thousands of his closest friends, and he's had access to the virtually limitless funds his parents provide.

For as far back as he can remember, Kevin has gotten whatever he craved without having to wait for it. It was never a matter of having to save up for something or even waiting to inherit his parents' fortune. So the thought of exploring a career never entered his mind—unless you can call skydiving, mountain climbing, sailing, and a variety of extreme sports a career. He didn't finish high school, but who needs a diploma? He'd never be flipping anyone else's burgers!

Parents who have been blessed with great wealth are often terrified that their young children will turn into overgrown adult children like Kevin, but these parents are often clueless as to how to prevent it. As we've discovered in earlier chapters, the key is to cultivate character assets while your children are young. With the foundation of a generous, caring spirit that is willing to give liberally and a prudent strength of mind that is able to save for future needs, your child is not likely to develop into a Kevin. But one of the most powerful tools for developing self-control and godly character is exactly what got Kevin into trouble—parents' giving their kids money.

MAKING ALLOWANCES WORK

For an allowance to have a positive effect on your children, you have to establish some broad principles of allowance management. With the right approach, an allowance can become a powerful tool in forming godly character in your kids while making them money-savvy at the same time.

Principle 1: Limit the Amount

An allowance that produces positive results is one that is intentionally tied to character development. Kevin, even at age twenty-four, is still getting an allowance—a huge one—from his parents. But in the sixteen years that his parents have given him financial assets, he has learned absolutely nothing. One reason is that the cash was so abundant that there were no limits on his spending. For an allowance to contribute to character building, you have to limit the amount. Give your children enough money to enable them to learn important lessons, but never give them enough to get into trouble. In other words, keep them hungry.

While this may sound mean, consider the fate of the typical goldfish. I've killed more pet fish than I can count by not wanting them to starve. Most children, when confronted with a tankful of colorful tropical fish or even a single goggle-eyed one, will have the same instinct. "Mom, Scaley's hungry! Can I feed him?" Left to the well-intentioned instincts of practically any kid, poor Scaley is doomed to a quick death by overfeeding. Likewise, you can doom your children with excessive generosity, especially if you give them access to large quantities of assets that they haven't been trained to manage appropriately.

What's the magic amount to give each kid, and how do we adjust the amount for age? While I've seen various amounts mentioned in semiauthoritative sources, I believe you should develop your own system for determining how much each child should get as he or she grows older.

Some parents would set the proper amount at zero. I know a wonderful family that has raised their children to an astonishing level of mutual love, generosity, and caring—without ever giving them an allowance. Even though these kids are the children of a successful surgeon and have had the blessings of country living and private schools, they were never overindulged. Their mom bought some of their clothes at thrift shops and ensured that every child had chores appropriate for his or her age. For the most part, they weren't shortchanged by not receiving an allowance.

But children raised in a no-allowance environment do miss out on an early exposure to the ABCs of money management. A time will likely come when they will have access to substantial funds for the very first time. Isn't it better to help them take financial baby steps while you're still there to train and guide them and to catch them when they fall?

Principle 2: Don't Pay for Household Chores

It's not a good idea to link allowances to the performance of household chores. Children need to develop internal motivations that don't rely on the promise of being paid. They need to find the simple sense of satisfaction in hard work well done. If you fall into the trap of doling out an allowance as payment for household help, prepare yourself for every simple request to turn into an unpleasant ordeal: "Justin, come help me rake these leaves." "Well, how much is it worth to you?"

In contrast, when allowances are freely given, we're in a position to model our own heavenly Father's generosity. We also have a great deal more moral influence in helping our children make wise giving, saving, and spending choices since the money wasn't derived from their own labor.

Also, try to avoid cutting off a child's allowance as punishment for unacceptable behavior. That discipline strategy might prevent other important lessons from being learned. What parent would dream of punishing his or her eight-year-old by saying, "If you don't shape up you won't be going to school for a month!" An allowance is another form of education, since it helps train kids in good character. So find other forms of discipline for wrongdoing.

When deciding on the best amount to give as an allowance,

consider whether you can package appropriate expenses into your child's allowance. When my kids were growing up, at the beginning of each school term my wife and I took them out to buy new school supplies. My kids loved picking out binders, folders, and pencils—everything a well-equipped student could desire. We wouldn't dream of making this an allowance expense, because we wanted to do everything we could to make the start of school attractive, interesting, and fun.

On the other hand, ongoing school supplies should be paid out of allowances. Budget the purchase of certain necessities into your children's allowance. The entire amount should not be available for buying whatever your children want. Make sure they have to allocate their spending to also take care of what they need. If they goof up, don't bail them out—make it a learning experience

Principle 3: Insist on Giving and Saving

It's essential that kids set aside a portion of their allowance for giving and saving. Receiving money regularly helps them cultivate a generous spirit as well as a prudent mind. Agree up front that they will devote a certain percentage to giving and another portion to long-term saving. Give them freedom in this area, albeit under your watchful eye.

For example, money dedicated to the church, homeless shelter, a particular missionary, or a Bible society may not be used to buy a new skateboard. Even if the money for charitable giving is still sitting in the giving jar, it's off-limits—and the same principle applies to various savings goals. Kids need to know that their decisions, while not completely irrevocable, need to have a degree of rigidity. Savings can be reallocated, giving can be reapportioned, but neither can be looted to meet current shortfalls due to poor planning or unwise spending.

Principle 4: Keep the Allowance at a Reasonable Level

As your kids get older, some of them will begin to earn substantial money through after-school jobs. In some cases it would be good to reduce that child's allowance in order to allow her earnings to cover certain expenses. But do this within reason. You don't want to undercut the incentive to work! High tax brackets discourage earning growth for adults, so why inflict a similar burden on your kids?

Other children may be heavily involved in sports, music, drama, debate, or other excellent activities. A good student who also plays on two competitive teams may have very little time for a part-time job. Don't penalize involvement in good activities—keep that allowance up at an appropriate level.

I often wonder what was in the minds of Kevin's parents when they allowed him unrestricted access to limitless funds. It's likely that they had no idea that they were dooming their son to a crippled character. All his life he'll find it impossible to defer gratification, and he'll find himself targeted by every conceivable variety of scam artist, drug dealer, and human leech. As parents, we owe our kids more—by giving them less.

When properly managed, an allowance has benefits beyond training in good character. A good strategy will also promote the art of keeping appropriate financial records. In the next chapter we'll see that a kid's never too young to begin learning the money-savvy skill of bookkeeping.

Chapter 20

I Am Justin's Checkbook

Bookkeeping 101 for Kids

Millenniums before the invention of index funds and the NASDAQ, an individual's wealth was measured by the number of cattle he owned. Even today, marriages in some parts of the world contain the element of a "bride price," which often is paid in the currency of cattle. Solomon, the wisest man who ever lived, knew the importance of keeping accurate records of one's assets, suggesting, "Be sure you know the condition of your flocks, [and] give careful attention to your herds" (Proverbs 27:23).

I suppose that sentiment was the motivation behind the profession of accountant! Still, many of us would prefer a weekly root canal to the task of keeping our financial records up to date. Despite the stereotypical negatives associated with accounting, everybody—especially our kids—needs to know enough to keep track of their money. If Justin starts the month with twenty dollars in his wallet, he should know what happened to the money by month's end.

Accounting is a valuable control to ensure that we actually have the assets we think we have. If our expectations don't balance with reality ("How on earth could that check have bounced? There had to be a few hundred dollars left in that account!"), then accounting helps us readjust our expectations ("I owe Uncle Sam *how much?*").

Do kids really need to know this? I'm not the only adult in America who was in my twenties before I knew how to balance a checkbook. I know a retiree who has lived his whole life without acquiring that skill. Kids, though, have no need for a few bottom-line accounting skills unless they fall into one of two groups: those who will enter adulthood wealthy or those who won't. If either of those descriptions fits your kids, read on.

Young adults who start off poor live off their wits and their entry-level labor. They need basic bookkeeping skills to make the most of their modest paychecks. Young adults with inheritances or other assets need a basic bookkeeping competence to avoid being cheated by their financial managers. Either way, there's a huge upside to teaching our kids basic bookkeeping skills and making it fun.

THE IMPORTANCE OF RECORDKEEPING

Just as ancient Sumerian accountants kept tabs on inventory with coded knots on a string, the first step is simply counting. That's not a challenge for normal children. "Alicia, how many scrunchies (a hair accessory) do you have?" When the objects being counted are of interest, children show surprising aptitude for evaluating quantities. "Justin, how many video game tokens would you prefer—the square root of twenty-five or the cube root of sixty-four?"

While basic arithmetic ability is necessary for bookkeeping, it's really the knot tying that counts. In modern terms, a Sumerian accountant tying those knots is equivalent to writing down the sums in an organized, useful way. How can we coax our children into acquiring these recordkeeping abilities as painlessly as possible?

If your child has a collection of any type, start there. Whatever is being collected—trading cards, dolls, coins, seashells—encourage your child to count them up every way possible. If it's trading cards, they can be inventoried by team, by player position, by the year the player entered the majors, in order of batting average; or for pitchers, by earned run average. In addition to counting, have your kids keep accurate records of what's in their collections. Be sure to provide whatever resources are needed, such as account books, fine-point pens, and other useful tools whenever a child shows the slightest need for them.

Another great introduction to bookkeeping comes as a result of charitable giving. By adding recordkeeping to the giving equation, your child can keep a cumulative record of what he or she has given over the years. If you want your child committed to a lifestyle of generosity, there are few things more motivating than knowing that he has made significant gifts over the years. Writing down various gifts and subtotaling them by organization or purpose also helps him understand the breadth of impact his gifts are having.

You can help your child keep similar record books related to his various savings plans. Whether a short-term savings target (for example, a new skateboard) or a long-term investment in stocks or mutual funds, a record book is a great place to keep track of current assets. If he owns stock, have him periodically update the value based on the current price from the daily newspaper. This gives your child a sense of ownership and makes these intangible assets much more real. And as long as the invested assets carry a sense of tangibility, the temptation to exchange them for some current purchase (cool sunglasses, for example) can be more easily kept under control.

By far the best tool for introducing accounting is to tie it into the allowance structure. Ideally, a child should learn at each stage of life how to account for the assets that God puts into his or her hands. As a very young child it is enough to just not lose those assets. "Justin, where are your new shoes?" "Beats me, Mom!"

As those assets become more sophisticated (such as real money), the goal is to help your child hang on to what he has until it is given away, saved, or spent intentionally—not just frittered away. I suggest encouraging a tradition where, as a parent, you hand over the allowance and your children immediately divide up those assets among giving, saving, and a spending account. Have Justin record the results. If he thinks you forgot to give him his allowance this week, have him check his ledger. A highly motivated record keeper will go so far as to write down how he used the spending portion of his allowance.

When you introduce the idea of recordkeeping, some of your kids will resist it wholeheartedly. In that case, the best you can do is to provide incentives. I've already suggested providing all the necessary accounting resources (for example, ledger books). Any reasonable incentive would be appropriate. For example, a parent could announce: "Next week at allowance time, whoever has kept a record of how this week's allowance was used will get a special trip to the skate park!" If this isn't enough of an incentive, perhaps the allowances are too large. Remember, when it comes to money, keep your kids hungry.

JUSTIN'S FIRST CHECKING ACCOUNT

When should a child get his or her first checking account? Most parents err on the "too late" rather than the "too early" end of the spectrum. Most kids (I was one) probably open their first checking account when they leave for college, which is about six years too late.

A much better alternative is to take your kids on their twelfth birthday (they're not yet a teenager, so they just might think this is a cool idea) to a bank that offers kid-friendly checking accounts. Open a student account (or some other low-volume, low-cost account) and fund the first deposit. Make it big enough to have some significance—perhaps fifty or one hundred dollars—because you're going to use it for leverage. The deal is simple: If Justin keeps his checkbook balance up-to-date and periodically balanced, the first deposit becomes his on his sixteenth birthday.

By this time all the play-bookkeeping should make keeping an orderly checkbook a piece of cake. The only trick is to walk him through reconciling his checkbook register with a monthly bank statement. Fortunately, almost every bank statement has printed on the back a form to help simplify the concept of reconciliation. After a few kitchen-table sessions where you work through it together, the job should become fairly easy.

As an ongoing incentive for your child to keep his account reconciled, consider doing the reconciling at some kid-friendly place (pizza or ice cream parlor), or go there to celebrate after each successful session. It might even be appropriate for you to make a small deposit in your child's account with each reconciliation. After all, we want to make sure the account isn't completely static.

Electronic Tools

As a modern, computer-savvy reader you may have been rolling your eyes at the thought of keeping old-fashioned paper ledgers and checkbooks. Why not introduce Justin to the joys of computerized bookkeeping, using programs such as *Microsoft Money* or Intuit's *Quicken*?

This is actually a good idea—*after* the basics have been learned with low-tech paper methods. Those computer programs are so good that it's possible to use them with little or no understanding of what's actually going on behind the scenes. That means they can rob children of the principles involved in keeping accurate records.

As Justin's finances become more complicated—and you're gearing up to send him off to college—by all means, transition to a computerized system. Go even further—make sure his checking account information can be painlessly downloaded into his financial software. After all, the goal is not to lock him into nineteenth-century bookkeeping methods, but to teach him the basics of accounting painlessly and thoroughly when that window of teachability is still open.

When you finally drop Justin off at college, stifling your sniffles and wondering what happened to your baby, don't worry. You still have one more shot at helping him get this financial thing figured out. In the next chapter we'll see how, through careful planning, Justin's college experience can help him become a competent, mature money manager in his own right.

A Practice Run for Adulthood

From Rug Rat to Rat Race

During a mission trip to Fiji in the summer of 1982, I visited the Suva harbor where I was entertained on a twenty-meter blue-water yacht. I've enjoyed sailing ever since I saved up and bought a Styrofoam-hulled Sea Snark when I was twelve—which I still have and still sail, by the way. But the vessel in Fiji was a mahogany-and-stainless-steel wonder. *It must be heaven to own one of these beauties,* I couldn't help but think. That's when my host brought me back to reality with a vivid, startling image of blue-water sailing: "Imagine spending your summer in a cold shower, tearing up twenty-dollar bills as fast as you can. That's the reality of yachting!"

Well, at least you get a suntan out of the deal.

The same money-shredding description could be used for sending your kids to college. You even get the occasional bucket of cold water in the face.

In the next section, I'll address some of the potential catastrophes (financial and otherwise) that we all want our college-age kids to avoid. For now, though, let's set our sights on the positive—the opportunities that the semi-independence of college life offers. This preamble to independent adulthood can enable our children to bridge the gap from rug rat to the rat race. We want our kids not only to assume the mantle of financial independence, but to wear it with style and elegance.

If we've done our homework well, our college-bound child will already have developed many positive character attributes. She'll be generous, thrifty, and largely immune to peer pressure. And she'll possess a well-developed ability to defer gratification. She'll know how to maintain and balance a checkbook, and she'll have a working understanding of long-term financial investments.

But up until now, all of this has been little more than practice. As long as kids are being housed, fed, and clothed by their parents, the impact of their financial choices is dampened. If they blow their whole allowance week after week, they're still not going to starve or go homeless. But when they're in college, our kids need to practice the skills they've learned in a way that will simulate real life. College is a great time to put the finishing touches on this whole mélange of character assets and practical financial skills. Unfortunately, many college scenarios don't naturally lend themselves to promoting that goal—so we'll have to engineer them.

LEAVING HOME FOR STATE U.

Consider a family of modest means. They send Justin first to the local community college to save on tuition and housing costs. He heads off to class every day, but he still lives at home. This situation is very little different from high school. Justin doesn't have to worry about paying rent, utilities, or car insurance.

Some might suggest charging Justin for sleeping quarters and the food he consumes. He could also be charged for a portion of the utility costs and for having his laundry done. This is a possibility, but it seems a bit harsh. A better option is to give Justin his educational funds in less frequent intervals and make him responsible for developing and implementing his college budget.

Imagine, for example, that you've budgeted a certain amount per year for Justin's first two years at the local junior college. Work with him to allocate those funds on a quarterly basis. Help him understand how that money has to be divided up to cover tuition, books, transportation, meals, a parking pass, and all the other expenses associated with college. Make sure you write the checks at the beginning of each quarter so that the most important expense—tuition—will always be paid, no matter how erratically the rest of the funds are distributed. While you want to continue to allow Justin to live with the consequences of his mistakes, you certainly don't want those mistakes to derail his college education.

But what if your family finances allow for a different educational scenario? Suppose Justin is planning to spend four years at a private university in another state. The Latin phrase *in loco parentis* means the university will function as a substitute parent while the beloved offspring is in their care. Of course, at nonreligious schools this is often understood to mean that the parents may pay all of Justin's bills but may not object to coed restrooms, sanctioned sexual experimentation, and a curriculum devoid of references to historic Christianity (except for the Crusades, the Inquisition, and the Salem witch trials).

In financial terms, however, it generally means that Justin will never see a bill, and you—the real parents—will see them in eye-popping abundance. When I went away to college I was blissfully unaware of how much my parents paid for tuition, books, housing, food services, student fees, lab fees, and the list goes on. Only now, standing in the shoes of a parent, can I empathize with the financial burden they bore—and they even bore it cheerfully!

But the student, wallowing in blissful ignorance, typically feels few of the financial blows resulting from his choices. I recall a dorm buddy whose parents had him on a full meal plan—but I don't think he ever ate on campus. He graced every off-campus pizza parlor and Italian restaurant between Durham and Chapel Hill, in effect soaking his parents double for food.

Many students casually drop courses just because they aren't getting the grades they hoped for. I, on the other hand, was too terrified of losing my student deferment from being called up for active military duty to even think of dropping a course! But I knew other students who slept through the first five weeks of classes before sauntering over to the registrar's office to fill out a drop slip, oblivious that their parents would have to pay the full price of a course for which the student attended not a single class.

What's the best way to engineer this situation to inject a note of reality into the student's life? One approach is the all-or-nothing reward method. During a moment of temporary insanity I once promised my son, Josh, that if he got a perfect score on his Scholastic Aptitude Test we would buy him a new car of his choosing. Fortunately he missed a few verbal questions, but he was intensely motivated for a brief time.

A college version of this would be to suggest that if Justin graduates in four years, with no needless extra expenditures, then he can have—ta-da!—a new car. This is an especially good plan if you had already intended to get your new graduate a present of this caliber. On the down side, however, the goal is too remote to have much effect on a kid's day-to-day motivation. "I feel like sleeping till noon" is a very real and present pleasure, while the promised prize is definitely pie-in-the-sky.

A more useful—and practical—approach is to set up your college-age child's finances so that they simulate as closely as possible what life is like in the work world, when a kid will be paying his bills out of his paycheck. This way Justin has a perfect opportunity, while still in college, to become aware of the true cost of living. And he has four years to practice before he has to do it in "real life." You can arrange this by setting up access to his educational funds with a two-signature check system. Justin keeps the checkbook, and each term he visits the bursar to square his accounts for tuition, room, and board. With a two-signature check system, rather than handing over the check to the bursar, he signs it and sends it with the appropriate support documentation to a parent for a second signature. The twice-signed check then is dispatched by return mail to the bursar.

As a thrifty parent, however, I'd rather funnel those hefty bills through an airline-mileage-earning credit card. But even if I went that route I would still insist on getting the bill through my child rather than directly from the college finance office. We're doing something like this with Josh, currently in a master's program in biochemistry. We authorized him to charge his tuition each quarter on our mileage-earning credit card—but he at least serves as the bagman. As far as his living allowance for rent and utilities is concerned, we send an amount to him in a check twice monthly—just like a real paycheck. His goal is to live wisely within those limits and apply all that we've taught him (or not) about financial management in the process.

While our children are drinking deeply at the font of higher learning (taking classes like History of the Silent Cinema and Literature of the Kalahari), they're also in a halfway house for adult financial management. They may make mistakes, and we'll feel the usual parental pressure to rush in and fix everything. Sometimes that's exactly what we must do, but other times we'll hold back so we won't rob them of the benefits of learning from the natural consequences of their actions.

The proverb I quoted in the last chapter—"Give careful attention to your herds"—goes on to warn that earthly wealth doesn't endure forever. As we raise our children to adulthood, we pray that they'll see money as God's gift to be given away, saved, and spent wisely so they'll become good stewards of God's assets. But there are no guarantees in raising children, and they might make numerous missteps before their adult character is formed.

Whether sailing a mahogany yacht or a plastic Sea Snark, we

need to help our kids steer around the navigational hazards that could sink them. In the next section we'll take a close—and sometimes difficult—look at the most common scenarios for the kinds of financial disasters to which almost-adults are prone and see if we can get them past the rocks with nothing worse than a scraped bottom.

PART VI

SURVIVING
FINANCIAL
DISASTERS

Chapter 22

The Driver's License

Turn Driver's Ed into Character Ed

There are few milestones in a parent's life that compare with the terror of watching one's offspring lurch off down the street at the wheel of a flimsy, overpowered rolling deathtrap—or whatever family car they've talked you into letting them drive. The pace of our children's growing-up years hits high gear when they get that most precious of near-adult documents, a license to drive.

None of us wants to see our babies grow up, let alone come to harm, and there are few more dangerous combinations than teenagers and fast cars. Even slow cars pose a certain threat. The thought of our son or daughter behind the wheel can merge in our minds with those horrible highway safety films we saw back in driver's-ed class. That shudder we feel should awaken us to one terrible reality about raising children: They aren't really ours!

And they never were. Our children, like our financial assets and our very selves, all belong to God. Just as we are stewards of the material possessions that God puts into our hands, our children are not really "his greatest gift" to us but are actually "his greatest loan," which he has entrusted to us. While we'll never lose the joy of the parent-child relationship (even as it matures into a strong adult-adult relationship), we need to acknowledge that our children's lives are in God's hands. The coming of age represented by driving is a perfect time for us to recommit our children to the Lord.

We can't hold back time, but we can design a strategy to wring the best possible outcomes out of this nerve-racking period. Now is a great time to make the most out of a few lingering opportunities to influence our kids. So set specific goals long before your child gets a driver's license. And start working on achieving those goals before the onslaught of adolescent hormones renders further advancement unlikely.

Your strategy should include three basic steps. First, make sure your kids begin driving as early as possible. Second, let them know that as long as they act responsibly, they'll have access to reliable family transportation. Third, help them understand the actual cost of automobile ownership.

Some parents, on reading that list, might object to the first two steps. "That's crazy! I'd prefer that my kid not drive at all, let alone when she's fifteen! And I don't know about promising ready access to the family car." Before you send me off to an institution, try to see the method to my madness. The three-step strategy is designed to make it easy for children to make good choices (remember the "Octopus Principle"?) and harder for them to make wrong ones. And when it comes to driving, we want them to consistently make very good choices.

GET THEM DRIVING EARLY

The first step is to have your teenager start driving as soon as possible. In most states, a kid can get a learner's permit at age fifteen. But the law stipulates that the teen can drive only in the company of an adult—in most cases, his mom or dad. This is prime time for parental influence in the life of a teen.

If you're not temperamentally suited to teach your child to drive, by all means hire a professional. My own parents recognized their limitations in this area (as a teen my father smashed up an unofficially borrowed car on his return from the license exam!), so they recruited a young man who for a living taught hapless teens to drive. As my instructor taught me to drive, even to parallel park with precision, he made a deeper impression about safety issues than my parents could have because he was a lot cooler. His opinions—when it came to driving and safety, at least—became mine.

LET THEM DRIVE OFTEN

Once your teens have a learner's permit, step out of the way and let them drive at every opportunity. Act as if you have all the confidence in the world that they'll drive safely and well. Pretend that they're your private chauffeurs, and give them as many hours behind the wheel as possible. And no backseat driving! Make your suggestions (which they'll see as criticism) infrequent and as mild as possible.

That six to twelve months of training is a great time to negotiate a "driver's contract" for when your child at last can drive solo. With our son, Josh, we negotiated all his responsibilities in advance: occasionally washing the car, doing his part to get the oil changed and see that other basic maintenance needs were met, as well as other responsibilities. We also spelled out the consequences if he failed to follow through. What would happen in the event of a speeding ticket? How about a second one? What if he should get a *third* one? Drawing from the rich experiences of my own teenage blunders, and trying to think of every eventuality (irresponsible or unsafe behavior, a drop in grades, etc.), we wrote a comprehensive contract[1]—and stuck to it when the inevitable happened.

TEACH THE COST OF AUTO OWNERSHIP

The thrill of driving the family sedan only lasts a short while with most kids—especially boys—and then their car-besotted minds begin to nibble at the idea of having their own wheels. Resist this tendency with all your might. Teenagers who get their own cars suddenly start pouring their money into a bottomless pit. Parents, often unwisely, subsidize this destructive tendency by shielding their kids from the true cost of car ownership.

A better solution is to give your kids access to the family car (or cars), and do it with style. Make them feel that they're getting access to a better, cooler car than they could ever afford on their own. If your family has the means, getting a car primarily for the children's use can help defuse a case of incipient hot-rod fever. If you can swing it, get a kid car that, even if it's not the safest car in the world, at least it's not the dorkiest.

Now your well-trained child, driving contract in the glove box of a family-owned car, is tooling around town, doing his best to impress other kids. Ah, blissful youth! Your teen still has *no idea* what it costs to drive so aimlessly on his parents' money. But as a parent who wants to raise money-savvy kids, you're going to teach him the financial realities of the automotive world.

Bring your teens into the mysterious world of the hidden costs of vehicle ownership—and make them do the math. I tend to regard use of family vehicles as another aspect of being part of a family. You don't charge family members for the use of the TV room or the kitchen, so why charge for using the family car? But without charging a fee, how do you help young Justin learn the true cost of automobile ownership?

One strategy is to make his use of the car dependent on his willingness to keep track of basic auto maintenance and to do some auto-related cost accounting. Have him keep an up-to-date ledger that tracks car expenses: scheduled maintenance, occasional repairs, gas, insurance, and—a big one—depreciation. In addition, put him in charge of seeing that all cars get oil changes every three thousand miles. He doesn't have to change the oil himself—or even pay for it—but he'll acquire valuable insights into the care of cars that will pay big dividends as he gets older. If he fails to stay on top of these responsibilities, restrict or curtail his access to the family cars.

Most teenagers, when they understand the full cost of owning a car, are willing to back away from taking on that burden prematurely. If yours is mule-stubborn, and nothing will change his (it's usually a guy) determination to buy a used VW for three hundred dollars and "fix it up," consider making it a joint project. Get a car for which do-it-yourself maintenance can be a learning experience (a VW is actually a good choice in that regard). Consider a sweat-equity arrangement whereby you pay for parts and your youngster learns the art of auto mechanics.

If the thought of our own flesh-and-blood offspring zipping around in a home-built jalopy doesn't make our blood run cold, we're probably not good parents. We need to learn to deal with our fears and reentrust our children to God who loaned them to us in the first place. When it comes to our kids' learning to drive, the best we can do may be to stand aside and allow them to spread their wings.

But won't they fly away? They may try—especially at college—so in the next chapter we'll look at another potential car-related disaster. Namely, should our children take a car to college? We'll see that there's a way to turn a kid's college car into a motivating force for better grades—really!

Chapter 23

Cars and College

It Doesn't Have to Be One or the Other

"Doctor Jake" had only had one goal since childhood—to become a physician. As a young boy, his play always seemed to be focused on diagnosing and treating his little friends, and his favorite toy was a real stethoscope from his uncle—a physician whom young Jake admired and hoped to emulate some day.

When Jake turned fifteen he acquired a new passion. He yearned to drive, but not just any car—he wanted to drive *his own* car. His parents didn't encourage this interest, but Jake had access to his savings, and as soon as he got his driver's license he became the proud owner of an aging muscle car. His parents insisted that he pay his share of the increased cost of liability insurance—an annual amount only slightly less than what the car was worth!

Jake lined up after-school and weekend jobs to pay for gas, insurance, and an endless stream of modifications and improvements to the car. He didn't have time to do the homework in college preparation classes, and he often did no better than a B in the less-than-challenging classes with which he filled his high school career.

By the time he graduated from high school, Jake's grades and lack of financial resources meant that the local community college was his only option. He realized that his chances of becoming a doctor had vanished. His teenage bout with car fever had ruled out the career that he had dreamed of since childhood.

But stop for a moment and run the tape back. Jake's story didn't have to end this way. Let's imagine that his parents helped him avoid the long hours devoted to after-school jobs that were necessary to cover the expenses of his muscle car. Instead, Jake drove the family car. He worked much less and studied a great deal more, and after he graduated, he was accepted into a university that offered an excellent opportunity to prepare for a career in medicine.

Now that Jake is ready to enter college, his parents have another big decision to make: "Should we let Jake take a car to college?" If he's going to live at home and commute to a community college, the potential for disaster is minimized. In that case, a car is usually necessary to get to class. But what if Jake's going away to college? Wouldn't a car give him the means to get groceries, run errands, and come home for vacations? Wouldn't a car be exactly what he needs to get the most out of his college experience?

In Jake's opinion, any loving and reasonable parent would actually *insist* that he take a car to college! But let me suggest another possibility. Jake does take a car to college, and he immediately finds himself amazingly popular. Since only one out of four freshmen at his school has access to a car, all of his friends (and he discovers that he now has many friends) learn that Jake is more than willing to share his blessing with one and all. He soon discovers all kinds of wonderful alternatives to attending classes and studying. Life at college is grand—one colorful whirl of friends, dates, and events, all facilitated by the fortuitous possession of a car.

As a card-carrying parent of a pre-college-age child, is this your dream for your offspring's college career? Do you want him or her to have unrestricted access to every off-campus delight that a car can make possible? I didn't think so.

Most freshmen need a car at college like they need another four years of acne. While there may be exceptions—and perhaps your children are the exceptions—the fact remains that the more access college students have to cars, the less likely it is that they'll achieve their potential. Even though your college freshman is seventeen or eighteen and the worst of adolescence is now blessedly in the past, there's still plenty of growing up to do. The lure of peer pressure becomes almost as strong as it was in the junior-high days, and a freshman is much more easily manipulated than that same child a couple of years later.

It's essential that your child realize the privilege and discipline that come with higher education. Anything that helps our children move in that direction should be encouraged. Remember all those school supplies we bought for our grade-schoolers? By all means, dig deep into your pockets and get your college-bound youngster a new computer and any number of books, tutoring, study-skill programs, library-research courses, or whatever else she needs. But don't fall for your offspring's pathetic pleas to be allowed to take a car to college.

If you have younger teens at home who still need a car, it will be easier to say no. "I'm sorry, but your three younger siblings still need the car!" But are there no situations when we should allow our offspring to have a car at college?

Since college is often a crucial time of transition from childhood to independent adulthood, there is a good case to be made for letting a child have a car at some point in his college career. While all kids are different, it might be motivating to write a new driving contract. The idea is this: If the student meets certain requirements, primarily academic but also including behavior and character-related issues, you will allow her to have a car during the last two years of college.

My wife and I found that this worked well for our two children, especially as they were separated in age by two years. While Laurie spent her two car-free years at college, Josh was enjoying the Subaru during high school. When we loaded up our minivan and installed Josh in his freshman dorm at UCLA, Laurie took possession of the Subaru. Since she was a junior and moving off campus, having the kid-car made sense.

This scenario helps the child avoid temptation in the impressionable early years of college, while providing a carrot in the form of a promised car in the final two years. By drawing up a car contract, you can still maintain a certain amount of leverage. You can insert a clause to the effect that the grades earned during the first quarter with the car must not be lower than the previous term, or the car comes back home. If your student understands that you're serious, that child will move heaven and earth to ensure that the car stays on campus. In other words, you have the potential to turn a study liability into a study motivation. (This assumes that you have access to your child's grades in college, a factor deliberately hindered by some universities.)

Of course, all this is contingent on family resources. In a later chapter I'll have more to say about college financing decisions, but I'd advise against providing a car in college if any portion of your child's education is being financed by loans. College loans all too often become a noose around a child's neck, and I'd rather see a student remain carless for four years than have him subjected to the burden of postgraduation debt.

One day our children's college graduation will come (possibly followed by grad school, medical school, or seminary), and they'll be considered full-fledged adults. They'll have earned the right to spread their wings and fly! If we raise them wisely, we can turn their adult selves over to the care of our heavenly Father with a sense of satisfaction and the knowledge of a job well done.

But what if something hasn't gone as well as we hoped? In the next chapter we'll see that with proper precautions, we can at least ensure that wayward kids don't have access to unlimited funds to accelerate their own destruction.

Chapter 24

If a Teen Goes Bad

How You Can Limit the Damage

There's something about a hang glider cutting through the sky that awakens a sense of wonder in spectators below. Many times I have glided over my old neighborhood in Southern California, killing time and altitude while getting ready to land, only to hear cries of amazement from the residents as they caught sight of the local daredevil.

"Why, that's nothing more than a big kite!" was a common sentiment. There's one really big difference, however, between a kid's kite and my hang glider: the string. A kite won't fly unless it's attached by a string to someone on the ground, while a hang glider would never get anywhere if it were tethered to the ground!

Kids are like kites—they are connected to us for a reason. They need limits, boundaries, and a sense of external control. Adults are like hang gliders—they operate under their own control, and they need to be free of the string-pulling manipulation of others, including parents. Problems arise when kids try to yank themselves loose from parental control when they're not yet ready to take full responsibility for the consequences of their decisions. In general, I'm a big fan of allowing the natural consequences of poor choices to teach kids lessons they won't soon forget. One of my seminary students surprised me once with this burst of insight: "Experience is a harsh teacher, but fools there be who will learn no other way."

There's no arguing that children go through various stages of foolish behavior. Consider, for example, the current fad of body piercing. On what rational planet would a massive tongue stud be considered cool? But we have a parental duty to shield our children from the most drastic consequences of foolish behavior, especially if their safety or health is threatened. I don't believe that the best way to teach kids to swim is by heaving them into the deep end of the pool and then stepping on their fingers when they try to climb out.

Sometimes kids need to be rescued from their poor choices, but an even better approach is to engineer their choices so the truly dangerous options aren't even on their menu. What are some of these "worst" choices? Fooling around with drinking or drugs. Dropping out of school. Shacking up with their girlfriend or boyfriend. Running away to become an exotic dancer in Las Vegas. And those are just a few of the possibilities.

Teenagers are concerned with establishing identities of their own, separate and distinct from their parents. This is a necessary step toward independent adulthood. But in the process, many teens go through a rebellious phase that poses a threat to their welfare. That's why parents need to make sure a teen's financial assets aren't used to fuel a self-destructive binge.

The Temptation of Financial Assets

It's my prayer that if you have focused on raising kids with kind, generous hearts and the habit of deferring gratification, then your teenagers' troubles will not set new records for inflicting parental misery. On the other hand, if you've been raising your children to give generously, save wisely, and spend carefully, then it's very likely that they have amassed significant assets. If you throw in things such as gifts from relatives, inheritances, and other liquid assets, they could have access to enough money to really get themselves into trouble.

To help protect your kids from themselves, you need to set appropriate limits on the access they have to their money. Let me make this clear: Your children's money (including stocks, collectibles, account balances) is theirs, not yours. Establish a high standard of accountability to ensure that their assets are never absorbed into yours. Part of being a faithful steward of your children's money is keeping it separate from your own.

That being said, if your children enter a phase of making disastrous choices, you don't want them to be able to accelerate their destruction by allowing them unrestricted access to their money. You need to put controls in place, much like the circuit breakers in your home's electrical panel. Most of the time you're blissfully unaware of circuit breakers, but when an electrical circuit in your home overloads, the circuit breaker pops open and interrupts the flow of current. Normally you're glad that electricity is available—but not if it's about to burn your house down.

Every significant financial asset your child has should have a circuit breaker. It needn't be an obvious one, just one that will enable you to pull the plug if needed. That's one reason I strongly support the idea that parents provide a safe, insured car for their kids—in the parents' name, of course—rather than allow a child to own a car. If a child becomes reckless in his or her driving habits, the parent can legitimately restrict or even prohibit access to the family car.

The same principle applies to finances. If a child receives an inheritance or significant gifts from relatives (often earmarked for education), the best solution (and one often required by law) is to put the assets into a custodial account. Let's imagine that for five consecutive years, Justin's grandparents gave him an annual gift of stock in the amount of ten thousand dollars. They might have a net worth sufficiently high that they're anticipating a problem with estate taxes. By giving stock to their grandson, they can take advantage of a loophole that allows them to make annual gifts of up to ten thousand dollars tax-free.

What should Justin's parents do with that first gift? They should strongly consider setting up a custodial account with a discount brokerage firm and fund it with the stock gifts. Make sure that a parent is named as custodian. Set it up so Justin doesn't have access to the funds until he reaches an appropriate age. The default age of access for such accounts is usually set at eighteen or twenty-one, but I recommend age twenty-five or later.

If your child turns out to be a levelheaded person with good financial sense, you can always give him access early. But if you don't set it up initially with these restrictions, he could gain access to it as early as age eighteen. And there would be nothing you could do—legally, that is—to stop him. He could choose to buy a motorcycle, drop out of school, and smoke up the balance in a marijuana-fueled stupor.

Even without the contributions of wealthy relatives, Justin might prove to be an aggressive saver and a savvy investor. Remember those first shares of stock he bought in companies that offered direct purchase of company stock? (See chapter 16.) Make sure that, while they're in Justin's name, you still have to sign off somewhere before he can sell them. If possible, move them into a custodial brokerage account as his assets accumulate.

"But It's *My* Money!"

None of these measures is intended to cause your children to feel less in control of their assets. In fact, the restrictions should be as inconspicuous as those circuit breakers that unobtrusively protect your home. But if your teen suddenly and temporarily loses all his or her good sense, you need to be able to pull the plug.

Now, a teenager could forcefully complain: "But it's *my* money! I should have a right to do whatever I want with it!" To which you calmly respond that yes, it is indeed her money, but you have a duty to not allow it to be used in a way that would harm her. If the money was given for a specific purpose—such as education—you can point out that as long as you're the custodian, you have a responsibility to ensure it is used for the purposes for which it was given. It does your kids no favor to provide them with financial assistance as they pursue a self-destructive path. And if they do turn back, at least those assets will be available for picking up the pieces.

One of Jesus' most memorable parables was that of the prodigal son. The rebellious son demanded—and was given—his share of his anticipated inheritance. After squandering it on prostitutes and parties, his poverty drove him homeward in repentance. The father welcomed him back into his heart as well as his home.[1] While we pray that our children will not become prodigals, we should take whatever steps we can to ensure as rapid a change of mind as possible—and it's clear that poverty worked wonders in the case of the prodigal son. We can exercise a similar influence by keeping a string on our teens' assets. They may scream and shout at the unfairness of it all, but sometimes love demands appropriate restraints. Like kites, our teenagers need that string to fly properly, but the time will come when the strings will be eliminated.

This chapter suggested a few catastrophic ways that our children can blow their future by making foolish choices. In the next chapter we'll examine a minefield just waiting to detonate at the skipping feet of our unsuspecting offspring. I'm referring to the minefield of credit-card debt.

Chapter 25

The Hot-Stove Principle

Teaching a Healthy Fear of Debt

When your children go to college, they won't lack for mail. Every day will bring a new preapproved credit card to their mailbox. And each offer will promise a low introductory rate. Banks and other financial institutions make a lot of money off consumer credit, and they know college students control a sizable chunk of America's liquid assets. Why wait to buy something several weeks or months from now when you can get it today? Just put it on your card!

Although we're accustomed to this pitch, putting everyday purchases on a credit card is a relatively recent phenomenon. Our parents borrowed money only for large purchases, such as a house. Then people started borrowing to buy a car, then major appliances. But still, daily transactions were handled with cash or by writing a check. You purchased groceries, gasoline, and clothing only if you had the money in the bank to pay for them.

The ubiquitous credit card, as we know it today, hadn't even been invented when some of us were born. But our kids can't walk across a college campus during orientation week without passing solicitors offering everything from free T-shirts to cell phones. There's just one catch: You have to sign up for a credit card. Of course, that doesn't mean you have to use it. Right.

Some students are smart enough (though a bit ethically challenged) to sign up as Mickey Mouse or Mahatma Gandhi. But most soon find themselves on the receiving end of a flood of applications, offers, and—eventually—bona fide credit cards. There's something infinitely alluring—even grown-up—to an eighteen-year-old about stuffing his or her wallet with all these exquisitely personalized symbols of massive purchasing power.

"Just because I carry them doesn't mean I'll use them," the college freshman rationalizes. "But they're nice to have in case of an emergency!" Of course, our kids have interesting ideas about just what constitutes an emergency. Who knows when an emergency might come along in the form of fabulous new makeup that wasn't available back home or a totally cool CD player that also plays MP3 files?

When college kids still lived at home it was easy for parents to intercept the daily stack of credit-card solicitations. Regardless of whatever postal regulations I may have been breaking, I screened my own children's mail and weeded out the weekly invitations to financial ruin. But with college-age kids living in another city, even another state, our mail-filtering options range from few to none.

Since a college student is now making his or her own decisions, far beyond the reach of parental oversight, we need to brainwash— I mean "educate"—our kids about the evils of debt long before they leave home. We want to instill in our children a healthy fear of debt. Surprisingly, all those credit solicitations coming to our homes can be pressed into service to help debt-proof our offspring. The key is to show them how to read the fine print. Instead of stuffing Justin's junk mail into the paper shredder, save it and turn it into a series of lasting life lessons.

CONSUMER DEBT 101

Picture this scene. During an ordinary family dinner you pull a crumpled credit-card solicitation from your pocket. You announce calmly, "Look what came in the mail today!" (It's best to begin this conversation using mail with your name on it. Otherwise, your daughter may resent the fact that you've been hijacking her postal assets.)

You scan it quickly and observe, "Well, it says here that these people want to give us money. Should we take it?" Kids—especially teenagers—love to play the devil's advocate. ("But tattoos don't *have* to be permanent. They have these lasers that…") But this time, *you* take the devil's side by arguing in favor of accepting the money.

"It's free money," you maintain.

"Dad, it's not *free*, you have to pay it back!"

"But we can spend it now, and pay it back later. Maybe in a few months. Maybe even next year."

"Duh! With *interest*. That's how they make their money."

"But it says here it's only a nominal interest rate, and the monthly minimums are very small."

You continue arguing the foolish side of the debate while your kids convince you that only a certified lunatic would fall for this bull. Even the dimmest child (and yours and mine are all way above average) will catch on to the educational nature of this kind of parental performance, sometimes in seconds. So feel free to shift gears and move on to explore all the fine print on this fabulous offer. As you read the squint print, help your children find the answers to these questions:

Who determines the interest rate?

Who has the right to change the interest rate at any time?

What events would trigger catastrophic bumps in the interest rate? (A late payment would be a common trigger.)

If you carried only a balance of one hundred dollars on an 18-percent card, and made only the minimum payment on your bill each month for a year, how much interest would you wind up paying? Since the minimum payment sometimes doesn't reduce the principal at all, the entire amount paid during the year could wind up as interest!

Make it a game to find the "gotchas!" in every credit-card offer. These range from the obvious ones, such as absurdly high interest rates, to the sneakier ones, such as those "convenience checks" the credit-card companies thoughtfully provide. Many consumers don't realize until they've used one that they've just made a cash advance against the credit card. And cash advances typically begin to accrue interest charges from the date of the transaction, not from the normal payment date.

The attitude that you want your kids to develop is one of incredulous skepticism. "How dumb do they think we are?" is the ideal response. Now is the time to bring out a simple financial calculator. They are included in computer programs such as *Quicken* or *Money*, and there are free Web-based versions that do the same thing. There's nothing like the ability to do some quick what-if calculations with interest rates to open a child's eyes to the true cost of consumer credit.

Credit or Highway Robbery?

Imagine paying $332 for an MP3 player on a credit card with an 18 percent interest rate. The monthly "minimum payments" can be as low as five dollars per month. With a financial calculator your child can see that it could take *thirty years* to pay off that purchase at five bucks a month. After ten years of paying the minimum, the debt remaining is still more than $325. Once again, the desired reaction should be an indignant "How dumb do they think I am?"

Before our kids leave for college, they need to understand what kinds of purchases are compatible with incurring debt. In general, it's always better to save first and spend later, as discussed in previous chapters. Using the previous example of a $332 MP3 player, if we had invested the monthly minimum payment of five dollars for thirty years at 12 percent interest, instead of having just paid off the long-gone MP3 player, we'd now have the price of a car— $17,474.82.

Borrowing should only be considered for buying an important item that will last. Typically, these are houses and cars. In both cases the lender has security and the borrower is exchanging his or her money for an increasing share of ownership in a tangible asset. It's true that cars depreciate, but they also perform essential services such as getting us to and from work to earn an income. A new projection TV with surround sound, in contrast, only gets us out of the easy chair to insert another DVD.

LESSONS IN DEBT AVOIDANCE

How can we drive home the danger of debt while our children are still around and reasonably impressionable? Occasionally our kids will ask us to lend them money so they can buy something they desperately want. "But Mom, if I don't buy these Pokémon cards *now*, I'll never complete my collection! And I know it'll be worth a fortune in just a few years." Sometimes it's a good idea to go along with their request and loan them some money. But use it as a learning experience. Draw up a written contract, establish a payment schedule, set an interest rate, and demand collateral.

"Sure, Justin, I'll lend you fifty dollars. Let's draw up a promissory note." In the note you specify the purpose of the loan: buying Pokémon cards. Specify the repayment terms, such as seven dollars per week for ten weeks. I realize that this is an absurdly high interest rate, and you would certainly be qualified to carry the label of "loan shark," but the idea is to create a painful object lesson. Be sure to spell out the collateral, and make it something that Justin really values. He'll try to pawn off something like his old skateboard or last year's video game, but don't fall for it. Insist on his current, hottest, and most treasured possession. Take custody of that asset immediately, and don't return it until the debt is paid off in full and on schedule.

"But he really loves his Discman. I wouldn't feel right taking it away from him," you whine. Well, tell me this. Does the auto lender feel remorse about putting the bank's name on *your* certificate of title? Does the mortgage company have pity on the poor borrower and release title to the house before the final payment is made? Does the loan shark wipe tears from his eyes before sending his goons around to break your fingers? The whole purpose of this exercise is to help Justin experience a little pain—pain at the beginning of the loan and pain for every day that the loan isn't paid off.

He's losing use of his most treasured possession for ten weeks, but that ache won't even compare with the agony if he defaults. Then he'll lose that possession forever! If necessary, give Justin opportunities to find ways to earn extra money to make his payments on time. These should be extra tasks, not his standard household chores. But if the due date comes and the loan is not paid in full, it's time for a settlement conference.

Sit down with Justin and go over the terms of the promissory note. Explain that he is now in default, and that means that you (the lender) not only have custody of his valued possession, but you actually own it. Explain that you're going to sell the collateral to pay off his debt. "But there's good news, Justin. Even if I don't get very much when I sell your Discman, I'll consider the debt paid in full."

Be prepared for a lot of screaming—from your kids, your spouse, and indulgent grandparents. No one wants to see Justin lose his treasured possession. So to avoid weeping and gnashing of teeth, brief the adults on what you want to accomplish and insist that they restrain themselves. Under no circumstances are they to bail Justin out.

After an experience like this, most children would respond to the question, "Say, kid, could I lend you some money?" with the same wary skepticism displayed by the victims of Tom Sawyer's fence-painting scam. You want to ensure that your kids never acquire a tolerance for debt. It should be painful from an early age, so the hard lessons won't easily be forgotten when your kids become grown-up college freshmen.

Imagine Justin's first week on campus. All the student organizations have set up booths to sign up new members. But that's not all. Plenty of credit hucksters are touting glamorous goodies in exchange for signing up for a "guaranteed" credit card. You can picture the scene. Justin looks. His face turns pale. His hands open and close in panic. He glances to either side of the looming threat, seeking an escape. He takes two steps backward, quickly turns around, and heads back to the dorm.

"Aah," you sigh with satisfaction and mentally give yourself a well-deserved pat on the back. God willing, you've instilled a lifetime wariness of debt in your pliable progeny. And you have deprived the credit industry of usurious income for generations to come. Well done!

But now that Justin's on campus and out of your sight, don't forget that he still needs your involvement. You no longer have direct control over every aspect of his life, but he still needs your direction as much as ever. In the next chapter, we'll examine how we can maintain our influence for a lifetime while gradually snipping the apron strings.

PART VII

CUTTING THE APRON STRINGS

Kids in College

Your "Semiadults" Still Need Parents

Here's an interesting experiment, but be warned. Unless you're pathologically bold, you probably shouldn't try this. The next time you're in a public place and surrounded by strangers, find an adult with a smudge on his face. Then whip out your none-too-clean handkerchief, spit abundantly on it, and say, "Let me get that smudge for you!" Then attempt to vigorously scrub your victim's face with your saliva-laden hankie.

Of course, you just don't do this sort of thing in polite company. You'd get punched or arrested or maybe both. But when your kids were toddlers, you *could* pull this off whenever they had a smudge. Parents can get away with just about anything when kids are young. You wipe their bottoms, correct their grammar, demand instant obedience, attempt to convince them (usually unsuccessfully) that green beans are actually a delicious dessert, and insist on a host of requirements that mentally competent adults would simply laugh at.

We parents think of our kids as still being kids no matter how old they are. So when they finally reach college age, we sometimes forget that they're no longer eighteen months old. While they were youngsters, we exercised authority and control. Now that they're adults, we have little more than mild influence. The trick is to cultivate our opportunities to exert that influence and not squander it on battles that won't matter years down the road.

One of the most helpful pieces of advice I received on the subject of raising teenagers came just in the nick of time—when my own children were entering that frightful period. Author and radio host Dr. James Dobson summarized what should be the primary goal for any parents whose children just entered the teenage years: "Just *get through* them." There's life on the other side of teenagerhood, and we parents need to choose our battles carefully in order to ensure that we'll still have a relationship—with its attendant influence—on the other side.

Sending kids to college puts us in a similar situation. The goal is to help our kids achieve independence, symbolized by choosing a career and becoming self-supporting adults. We want to continue to have a relationship with our adult offspring, but the college years are a minefield of prospective disasters, each of which could disrupt our relationships with our adult children permanently.

Some of those explosives were triggered well before your child arrived on campus, often by choosing an inappropriately expensive college or having inadequate savings set aside to cover expenses. I know a young professional who will be saddled with college debt for decades. She blames her parents for sending her to an ultra-pricey school and then sticking her with the bill. If you've paid attention in previous chapters, this shouldn't happen with your kids. Let's assume that little Angela is attending a well-chosen school and that the financial assets are in hand to complete a four-year degree. Sounds like everything's under control, right?

Maybe not. One night you get a phone call. "Dad! I'm going to save you a *ton* of money. I'm going to move off campus! Sure, it will mean commuting—but only about forty miles—so there's no problem, right?" Wrong!

Or consider this one from Noah, your sophomore son. "Mom, I'm going to do my junior year in Europe!" Never mind that it will cost half again as much as a year at his home campus. And don't worry that the resulting financial shortfall during Noah's senior year will mean taking out a hefty loan to enable him to graduate on time. And will those credits in medieval architecture and conversational Italian really fit into Noah's biochemistry major?

Or let's listen in on yet another hair-graying phone call from your daughter Maya, a senior. "Dad, I've met the boy I love, and we're going to move in together. We found a darling apartment that will even save you money!"

WHAT ARE THE OPTIONS?

Arrgghh! I can't remember which insect routinely eats its young, but phone calls like the above cause me to reflect warmly and appreciatively on the humble common sense of that creature. Since cannibalism isn't an option for human parents, it's helpful to make a list of our real-world choices. Our college-age kids still need our input, and their character still has moments of malleability, so here are three situations in which we can make those final tweaks.

Occasional Lapses of Judgment

College students are prone to commit regular but short-lived lapses of good judgment. When you become aware of these, employ the time-honored tactic used by generations of responsible parents: the talking-to. But make sure it's done in a casual way.

The informal talking-to should be reserved for matters where your superior parental wisdom and experience detect a problem that your child might not recognize. For example, you shouldn't waste your ammunition criticizing your son's choice in music, hairstyle, or other largely irrelevant cultural matters. In fact, you can sometimes get the same effect by surprising Caleb with how informed you are on the latest doings of his favorite group ("Say, did you hear that Sick Puppy's new CD is coming out next week?") or suggest that he'd look really great if he tinted his hair orange with purple streaks.

Make sure you reserve your informal influence to use the same way you would with a coworker who's about to make some serious blunder. "Ed, I've got to tell you—I bought that same coffee maker last year, and it was a complete loser." Adults don't tell adults what to do (law-enforcement officials and employers excepted), so you need to learn to interact with your college-age children the same way. Friendly, low-key advice is always more welcome than authoritarian pronouncements.

Let's suppose you discovered that Caleb was occasionally sleeping late instead of going to class. That's an occasion for using informal influence. As a parent, you'd probably be inclined to lay down the law. ("I'm not paying good money so you can get your beauty rest!") Consider instead a more collegial approach that treats Caleb as an adult. "Getting up is tough for me, too, even after all these years. Have you considered setting the coffee maker the night before? That first eye-opening cup really helps me get the day started."

But what about Maya's proposal to save money by moving way off campus and adding a forty-mile commute to her life? That one certainly warrants an informal talking-to. She needs to know that you would rather see her succeed in her education, and it's hard to do that from another part of the planet from where your college is located! Besides, it's doubtful that there's even a net savings when the cost of commuting is factored in.

Really Bad Judgment

When you're talking about college students, occasional lapses can sometimes turn into serious problems, and when they do it's time to bring in the medium-caliber artillery. In other words, sit down for a *formal* talking-to. This should be reserved for serious practical issues (as opposed to decisions with serious moral consequences, which we'll deal with next).

The formal talking-to should begin by clearly defining the problem in terms of exactly what's wrong with the suggested course of action and what the consequences would be. Noah's desire to spend his junior year in Europe would justify a formal talking-to. If possible, this should be conducted in a face-to-face discussion in some comfortable setting. With my own kids, we've found family restaurants to be a good location for these kinds of confrontations. Being in public helps keep everybody on their best behavior.

The goal is to help Noah understand the consequences of his happy-go-lucky yet costly scheme to take his junior year in Europe. Treat him like an adult. Give him the figures and show him the financial ramifications of pursuing his proposed course of action. Even if your personal finances would allow him to do what he's proposing, would it be wise in light of his character and personality? There are far more distractions in Italy than there are back home. Could Noah concentrate on his studies when the Riviera and the Alps, not to mention Rome and Florence, are constantly beckoning? If finances are a real issue, insist that he buy into the solution. Could Noah get an on-campus job immediately to build up cash that will help offset his extra junior-year expenses?

Whatever the situation, the objective of the formal talking-to should be to help your nearly adult student stop thinking in a childish way. "If this blows up in my face, Mommy and Daddy will fix it" is inappropriate thinking for a college student. They need to begin thinking in an independent and responsible way. "Hey, if I pursue this course of action it could have some rude and painful side effects."

In effect, you're putting Noah on notice that you plan to hold to your current position when it comes to finances. If he goes to Italy, the extra expense will cut into his senior-year funds, and he won't be able to graduate on time. And you're not going to chip in more money next year. That way, he can do the math himself. He'll have to get an extra job, take out a loan, or graduate a year late. Don't insist on an immediate resolution, and don't compromise.

Sometimes a dose of reality drives a stake through the heart of an impulsive idea.

Moral Peril

But what if your child's plan goes beyond mere bad judgment? What if it's a morally dangerous plan? Maya's proposal that her parents subsidize a live-in arrangement with her college boyfriend is morally catastrophic. This one calls for the heavy artillery. The goal is to draw a proverbial line in the sand, and it should be used only if your young adult offspring is asking you to violate your own moral principles.

I suggest arranging a face-to-face encounter similar to a formal talking-to. First, make sure you correctly understand what your child is proposing. "In other words, you and Bill would be sleeping together as if you were married?" Assuming that you do understand, your goal should be to clearly explain the moral nature of your objection and the consequences for your daughter. "Maya, you know we believe that God can only bless a sexual relationship within marriage, so you need to know that your mother and I would never finance that lifestyle choice. You're an adult, so you make the call. But if you choose that living arrangement, we'll no longer be covering our share of your college expenses."

The laying-down-the-law confrontation will be painful for everyone. Maya will feel judged and manipulated, and you'll feel guilty for not instilling your moral values more effectively when she was younger. The outcome can be negative. Maya may ignore you, drop out of school to support her shack-up partner, accidentally get pregnant, or contract a sexually transmitted disease. Despite all this, do what you can to maintain a loving relationship with her.

After all, she'll always be your daughter. But you also need to make sure that the issues are clear and that any negative consequences will be the result of Maya's choice.

Painful as this sounds, it may be the final wrench necessary to jerk our offspring from adolescence into responsible adulthood. Being an adult means having to make difficult choices, and sometimes college students gain wisdom only by making foolish choices and then experiencing the consequences. When our toddlers had smudgy faces, we could fix it with a spit-moistened hankie, and they would stand there and take it. College kids, however, need to be treated as what they are becoming—independent adults.

Even then, however, we don't do them any favors by financing their poor choices. Let's pray that they arrive safe and sound at graduation day. Their shiny faces, academic robes, and interviews with eager corporate recruiters are all pointing to a successful future as independent adults. Our faces will beam with pride at what our offspring have accomplished, and we'll glow with hope at what their future holds. But will we still have a place in their future?

How can we make the transition from parents to whatever it is that we become when our kids have launched their careers and achieved financial self-sufficiency? We never stop being parents, but we need to learn new ways of relating to our adult children. That's the subject of our next chapter.

Emptying the Nest...

Without Chucking Out the Kids

I wasn't a jogger at the time, but I admit that I was enthralled by reading rapturous descriptions of the joys of running. Jogging devotees spoke of the runner's high, which sounded fun, legal, and healthy. And they described how once they started running, they never wanted to stop. They said they felt as if they were floating in a calm, pure place far from the worries of this world. If simply going for a jog did all this, how could I resist?

I couldn't, of course, so I started jogging. Bring on that runner's high! I wanted to jog right into the heart of that calm, pure place the running enthusiasts couldn't get enough of. I didn't find it the first few times I went for a jog, but not to worry. I realized this sort of thing would take time. So I kept jogging, hoping with every step that I'd soon enter the realm of the runner's high. Instead, I'd come home with aching arches and projectile sweating. During the last half mile of my runs, I craved *not* running with an unspeakable yearning. By far the best part of my daily run was the hot shower and clean clothes that followed the ordeal.

If you stop and think, parenting is a lot like jogging. Sometimes you wish you *could* quit. While we can become parents by adoption, there's no easy way to divest ourselves of the offspring when they move through their most objectionable phases. But those phases pass, eventually. Your kids end up like butterflies emerging from what were once slime-filled cocoons. Teenagers grow up, spread their wings, and fly into the future. The great news at the end of this long struggle is that we can send our kids into the world as well-educated adults, earning their own living and making an important contribution to the world. We multiply our rejoicing if our children also enter adulthood possessing godly character and sprouting the first shoots of financial wisdom.

That's when we're tempted to sit back and take it easy, believing that our years of parental responsibility are over. Although our kids are now working and supporting themselves, that doesn't mean our task is complete. It's true that our interactions with our adult kids must evolve into a peer relationship, but this change also brings new needs and responsibilities.

INFLUENCE, NOT CONTROL

Once our kids become adults we have practically no control over their decisions. But we can continue to have a great deal of influence in their lives. Do you remember Dr. James Dobson's wisdom regarding the teenage years? "Just get *through* it," was its boiled-down essence. In other words, we should do our best to keep the relationship functioning, because that's the only leverage we have to influence our kids during the hardest times. Maintaining influence without attempting to impose heavy-handed control is one of the skills we continue to employ as parents of grown children.

One way to exert influence is to tap into the power of modeling. Even when your kids are adults, modeling remains the best way to get their attention and make an impact. So don't get sloppy in your personal life. Continue to be the kind of person you want your children to be. You no longer have to focus on molding the character of your children, so why not focus your energies on growing in your own character and walk with God? Seek out areas where you can give strategically and generously. Find ways to be involved in expanding God's kingdom and meeting the needs of his children. Demonstrate integrity and honor in every area of life. Grow in your understanding of what it means to be a child of God.

In your personal finances, continue to live on less than you make, and give generously and save wisely out of what's left. Remember that little eyes are still watching what you do far more than they're listening to what you say.

A second way to continue influencing your adult children is to dispense advice only when asked. It takes a lot of forbearance to keep quiet when you are pretty sure that you could, with just a few words of wisdom, set your kids back on the right course. Don't do it! And when grandchildren come along, put an extra layer of duct tape over your mouth, especially when it comes to offering advice on any aspect of raising children.

If we don't gratuitously tell our kids how they should deal with their own kids or their unreasonable bosses, how to negotiate with a transmission repair shop, or where and how to take their vacations, they're *much* more likely to ask us. And when it comes to exercising influence, answering a question is always preferable to volunteering a parental opinion.

ONGOING FINANCIAL TRAINING

In addition to exerting influence, we can initiate efforts that will provide tangible opportunities for our grown-up kids to grow in financial wisdom. Just as we did things to make it easy for our young children to do the right thing (remember the "Octopus Principle"?), we can continue to set up situations that will help our adult children learn to manage their assets. One of the best ways to do this is to give them gifts. Like our heavenly Father, who generously gives us everything, we can demonstrate openhandedness not only by giving to God's kingdom, but also by passing on our inheritance a little bit at a time while we can still influence how our children will use it.

This early distribution of part of your kids' inheritance has a second benefit. Giving away part of your estate while you're still living helps you dodge some taxes, as the tax code is very friendly to gifts. You can currently give ten thousand dollars per year to each family member with no tax consequences to them. This is a great way to pass along investments that have appreciated greatly over the years and would otherwise be subject to capital gains tax.

Restricted Gifts

If you have the financial means, try to make the first gift in a way that has some learning goals explicitly connected to it. Consider this offer to a married daughter and her husband: "Your mother and I would like to encourage you to set up Individual Retirement Accounts (IRAs). We'd like to fund the first year—that's two thousand dollars for each of you." Go on to explain that you want them to use this gift to research good mutual funds or stocks so that they'll have a high degree of buy-in on the project.

By choosing to help fund an IRA, you are putting the cookies out of reach. In other words, your kids can't just dip into their IRA funds whenever they want to buy a speedboat or a cabin at the lake. Consider making this an annual gift. But you want to encourage them to develop habits of thoughtful investment and generous giving, so if they do well with this first step, consider giving them a gift with unrestricted access in a following year and see what they do with it.

Unrestricted Gifts

A money-savvy adult child will benefit greatly from receiving an asset with no strings attached. Unlike the IRA mentioned previously, this type of gift comes from a parent with no restrictions. The child has full access to it.

You can do this by giving shares of stock. Let's say you're all sitting around the Christmas tree. After the gifts have been opened, you hand your young adult offspring an envelope containing the certificate for a block of stock. "Here—we wanted you to have some General Electric this Christmas." But now comes the hard part. You have to stand back and watch what they do with it. You hope they'll hold on to most of the shares so the stock can gain in value. But they may use the assets differently. It will be a bad sign if your kids quickly book a Caribbean cruise, buy a hot tub, and trade their two-year old minivan for a hot BMW. On the other hand, rejoice if they choose to give some, spend a little, and thoughtfully invest the rest.

Throughout life you can encourage your children to do the right thing through giving judiciously timed gifts. This can become a great way to help them fund their children's education, and it diminishes the estate tax burden when one day your children will inherit your assets. But speaking of inheritance, keep reminding your children that you don't plan to leave them much. Point out that there are many catastrophes in life that can reduce a large potential inheritance to little more than a few heirlooms and a handshake from the family attorney. And why rob them of initiative and motivation by suggesting that their own financial management could ultimately prove irrelevant since they are likely to inherit a bulging portfolio of assets when you die?

Stress that these occasional gifts are, in fact, their inheritance, and they would be wise to invest them carefully. In fact, take every opportunity to assure them that financial success in life is dependent on their living out the godly character that you worked so hard to instill in them.

What to Avoid

As you continue to exercise influence, but not control, over your adult children, there are two major hazards to avoid. First, never use your God-given assets to exert improper pressure on your children. A parent should never approach an adult child and say: "Son, I'm thinking of giving you a significant stock gift this year, but not if you plan to go ahead with your marriage to so-and-so." Either give the gift or don't give it, but never link it to your child's bowing to your demands.

Second, you should feel no compulsion to fund an immoral or useless lifestyle. Remember Kevin, the twenty-four-year-old dropout whose only skill was spending his parents' assets? While I believe God blesses families, and some of the assets God gives us can be passed on as a blessing to our descendants, God's money should not be given to family members to be squandered on an ungodly lifestyle.

THINGS OF ETERNAL VALUE

One day our earthly lives will come to an end. As we approach the later years of life, it becomes more apparent that the things that the world values most—money, property, power, prestige—have no ultimate meaning. Our worldly wealth is merely symbolic, and at the gray-haired end of life, we may realize that it's all Monopoly money anyway.

Ultimately each of us will stand before the Lord with no assets beyond the gold, silver, and precious stones representing a redeemed life lived wisely.[1] On this side of heaven, it's our privilege to use the portion of God's wealth that he lends us to build something lasting into the lives of those we love. Our kids are eternal, and the character we instill in them will have an eternal effect on their lives and in the lives that they touch.

Once the nest is empty, we transition into a nonparental mode. This can be a difficult shift, but it leads to a rewarding adult-adult relationship with our kids. We serve in a new role as loving peers, sounding boards, and friends to our adult children. If we've done our job well, we can rejoice that our adult children are savvy money managers as well as godly individuals.

I can think of nothing more fulfilling at the end of my life than this: My heavenly Father looks approvingly on the children he so briefly entrusted to me, and then he says to me: "Well done, good and faithful servant!"[2] I pray this will be my experience and yours as well.

Notes

Introduction

1. The English language has amazingly few really useful synonyms for the word *child*. I have unashamedly chosen to use the word *kid* for this purpose, knowing full well that there are many who believe (as did my late grandmother) that "kids are young goats, not children!" While grating to the ears of purists, virtually all modern English dictionaries count the word *kid* as an informal synonym for *child*. It might be some consolation to the stickler that the etymology of *kid* links it to the Gothic root *kin*, which, when it entered English from the Scandinavian language in the ninth century, may have had as much relevance to children as to goats. On a related issue, some perfectionists also insist that "one *raises* crops, but one *rears* children." I also go on record (dictionally speaking) that modern usage allows that children can be "raised" as well as "reared."

Chapter 1

1. J. Raymond Albrektson, *Living Large: How to Live Well—Even on a Little* (Colorado Springs, Colo.: WaterBrook Press, 2000). See http://LivingLarge.Albrektson.com.

Chapter 9

1. While the author of Ecclesiastes identified himself only as "the teacher," Solomon has traditionally been considered the author.

Chapter 16

1. The amount of cash I found in the jar was approximately $288, which would grow to $55,210, assuming an interest rate of 11 percent compounded monthly for forty-eight years.

Chapter 17

1. Would you like to know more about Griffin? See *What My Dog Has Taught Me About Life* by Gary Stanley (Honor, 1999).

Chapter 18

1. "While entertaining and well-written, do we really want to perpetuate the notion that those who do not contribute to society are thereby disqualified to share its common wealth? Folk tales like the 'Little Red Hen' encapsulate and perpetuate increasingly irrelevant bourgeois values from the past. Perhaps we need a new version, in which the hoarded product of the hen's industriousness is equitably shared with the other less-fortunate barnyard animals." (a review of "The Little Red Hen" found on Amazon.com)

Chapter 22

1. You can examine Josh's contract at my Web site: http://MoneySavvyKids.Albrektson.com.

Chapter 24

1. See Luke 15:11-32.

Chapter 27

1. See 1 Corinthians 3:10-15.

2. See Matthew 25:23.

About the Author

Ray Albrektson has been on the staff of Campus Crusade for Christ since 1974, following four years in the U.S. Air Force. He and his wife, Kathy, began their Crusade service in campus ministry in Florida and Indiana, and since 1986 he has served as an associate professor in New Testament at the International School of Theology. Although based near Rancho Cucamonga, California, the school has branches in Africa and Asia, as well as extension programs that have taken Ray on teaching trips to more than twenty countries.

Ray earned his bachelor's degree in physics at Duke University in 1970. While he was pursuing a master of divinity degree, his interest in finances led him to focus his thesis on the relationship between Christian workers' attitudes toward giving and their sense of financial adequacy. He went on to earn a doctor of theology degree in New Testament studies at the Asian Baptist Graduate Theological Seminary in the Philippines while helping to plant a branch seminary in that country.

In *Living Large: How to Live Well—Even on a Little,* Ray described how he put his biblical insights into practice. Ray and Kathy have lived joyfully on a meager income, saved for their children's education and their own retirement, and given generously to God's work. Ray says that if "poor missionaries" can live successfully and joyfully by following the principles in this book, anyone can!

Although academic credentials are important for correctly understanding biblical financial principles and character education, Ray believes his two best credentials are his adult children. Ray and Kathy's daughter, Laurie, is on the staff of Campus Crusade for Christ with her husband, Chris. Josh is a biochemistry graduate student at UCLA.

Learn more about the Albrektsons at http://www.albrektson.com, or visit their Web site at http://MoneySavvyKids.Albrektson.com.

Printed in the United States
by Baker & Taylor Publisher Services